THIS

BOOK IS

NOT

FOR YOU

Purposely written for me,
but may be life changing for you.

by

Carole Boudreau, NHP

This edition is published by
That Guy's House in 2018

www.ThatGuysHouse.com

hey,

Welcome to this wonderful book brought to you by That Guy's House Publishing.

At That Guy's House we believe in real and raw wellness books that inspire the reader from a place of authenticity and honesty.

This book has been carefully crafted by both the author and publisher with the intention that it will bring you a glimmer of hope, a rush of inspiration and sensation of inner peace.

It is our hope that you thoroughly enjoy this book and pass it onto friends who may also be in need of a glimpse into their own magnificence.

Have a wonderful day.

Love,

Sean Patrick

That Guy.

Tables of Contents

FOREWORD

I'm writing this part of the introduction, only a few minutes after I was Skyping with my publisher. My contract is being created and will be sent to me as soon as possible, then it will be signed within the next few days. I am so excited right now. It feels like I am walking on clouds. Who would have guess that little old me would one day publish a book?

It all started last December, when I was in between jobs. There I was, just turned 59 years old, not really quite understanding what was happening at that time. It seemed that I still didn't have a handle on life. Of course, in the past 12 years there had been a very big improvement. However, I quite still didn't find the right recipe for Carole.

My recipe!!! Those words moved something inside of me. All of a sudden, I was writing at the speed of light, all the things that needs to be done when Carole is down, and the "how to" get those things back on track. That's right! A book that will help me get out of my slump in a faster easier way. Why not? So within 18 days, I wrote this book.

Also within that time frame, I fell upon a Dr. Michael Beckwith[1] YouTube service and fell completely in love with the way he delivered a sermon. He also incorporated meditation in his service and that really worked for me.

I have been an avid follower of Dr. Joe Dispenza[2] for the past 12 years. However, I never could get into his ways of meditating. So, Dr. Beckwith's meditations became the missing link of my recovery book sessions.

Each person has their own Guiding System. You have to trust It. I sure didn't always. But in the past few months, I have come to bow down and honor Its revelations.

From this book I wrote in December 2017, to getting into Dr. Michael Beckwith's meditations and services, to going to Agape Revelation 2018 in California, USA, to manifesting a drive to a coffee shop after the first service on Sunday morning at Agape International Spiritual Center in Culver City, USA, and in meeting a publisher at that convention, I have accepted that I do manifest my destiny through the help of the Universe's pulls and tugs. And, for some reason, it is going at a very fast pace right now.

This book was written for me, yes. However, I have rewritten it with enough space for you to write and create your own recipe to a good life. Remember, the life that you want for yourself is not to compliment others. Although others are showing you different ways of going about your life, your plans and your life is not theirs. Sure, you will have some bumps and pot holes along the way. But, what happens is meant to be to create your story.

This book might have some controversial subjects

that you might not agree with. However, you need to understand that this book was at one point written to help one soul: "me". And then, I rewrote it so that you can also benefit from it. It is to help you, step by step, to regain your health, your mental focus on things, and understand what your true wealth is: "you".

So, don't hesitate in taking a few minutes here and there and meditate on what your potentials and dreams are. I have put enough space so that you can write your personal opinions, ah-ha moments and any questions that you may have that you would like to ask the Universe. Believe me! It does listen and it does answer back. We are just too busy to slow down and listen.

I would suggest that you get a pen or pencil, a highlighter and some post-its, and make this book yours. Write notes in the spaces provided or wherever you want. Highlight what you believe you should come back to or your AH-Ha moments. Use the post-it for book marks, so you can flip back to a favorite place. This is usually what I do with books. I don't read them. I devour them... lol.

Have fun with this book. Make it yours and also make it your passage to a brand new awakening.

And now, turn the page to a completely different way of looking at life.

INTRODUCTION

So, how do you create a book? I have been on this quest now for the past few months. I believe that if I write down what I need to know to help me regain my joy, then, whenever I would be down and out, I would just pick up the book and read a few chapters and say: "Ah-ha, that's what I forgot!", and move on from there. Something similar to breaking the glass in case of fire, my book would be "read in case of turmoil"... lol.

So, what do I put in my book? Well, one thing that I had decided not to put in this book is anything pertaining to my past that would make me blue, and that is a lot. Isn't it funny when you meet someone, the first few questions they start with are: "Who's your father and mother?; where were you born?; who are your brothers and sisters? They are only trying to associate you to something or someone else. They have not yet understood that you are a unique person. They seem to not have the capacity to see you for what you truly are. How about asking the sublime questions: "Are you happy? What makes you happy? What do you do to make you happy? Or, anything related to happiness so that the person you are conversing with has a glimpse of what happiness is.

I knew for a long time that I needed to be different. I needed to change. I mean physically change: Lose some weight AND rewire my brain.

Dr Joe Dispenza showed me what needs to happen in the brain to create such changes. I also understood how it needs to change: by monitoring and being aware of my emotions – the ones that have always been driving my life. His simple explanations of how it works really helped me.

It seems that I was going from one teacher to the other. However, I found my uniqueness by tweaking everyone's program to fit my personal spiritual development. This is very important for me. Dr. Beckwith touches what I truly believe. He has a unique way of reaching inside of you, to your true self, and pull out your greatness. Dr. Dispenza gets the scientific answers, and Esther Hicks[3] – the Teaching of Abraham – is true connection to the Source.

Now that I know the why it should be done, and the how to do it, I feel very confident about my life journey and what I can bring to this book and hopefully to this world, even though I still have a bit of fear as to how and when I will achieve it. It is a day to day adventure and believe me it is very exciting. **But I also learned that the achievement is not necessarily the most important in this adventure. It is the Journey**.

I had hit a wall, my spiritual wall, in 2014. I was seeking answers but couldn't find them. I was deaf to some guides, not because I didn't understand but it didn't jive with my true self. Dr. Beckwith is what makes my AH-HA moments go wild.

For me to make my vision come forth, I need to change, and in changing I mean physically (lose weight), mentally (rewiring my brain), spiritually (finding my peace within my soul and others who feel the same way as me).

So, not much from the past will be in this book, because the past is the past. You can learn from the past, build from the past and forget about the past – for those who can. The past is not a subject that a lot of people like to go into, unless you are addicted to your past, which is absolutely possible. I was one of those people.

Since I am writing this book specifically to help me get back on track, let's enumerate a few things that I do seem to have some trouble going through, and maybe a few of you might correlate with what I am about to write.

> *Why the heck am I here for? Is there a God? Why are people so mean? Who should I listen to? What truly drives us? And what part does the body has to do in this? What is the mind? What is the soul?*

Many books have been written on all of these subjects. However, not everyone speaks to me the same way that it would speak to you.

I have a journey that has started at the beginning of 2005 – I know, I wasn't going to speak about the past, but this part doesn't make me blue – and that is when I have found out that there is something bigger than ourselves out there and It also is part of all of us, or should I say that we are all part of It.

So, this book will be all about faith, hope and love (joy), which love (joy) being the most important of all. Joy is at the top of the list of all emotions you can dish out. I will be relating more about joy in this book because a lot of people cannot grasp love, or are mistaking it for something else. It is a word that is greatly misunderstood, like God. Some people relate love to sex and it is not the same. Some also relate God to a white bearded man who lives in the clouds. We will be discussing these in great detail in some chapters to come.

Events, good or bad, tend to make you forget the principal things in life. It is important to have some markers that bring you back on track. This is why I decided to write this book. I tend to get off track... often. Doesn't take much: a bad job, a relationship gone wrong, a co-worker giving you some hardship, death of a loved one – that's a bit more than much though– and loneliness. You can easily add to this list but I hope that you get the picture. When I get off track, I tend to go to the other end of the stick where despair, sadness and loneliness live. And, sometimes it takes me a long time to get out of that slump. However, I have found a way to get out of it faster and that is where my book comes into play. So, if I tend to forget about how magnificent we are as human beings, I quickly read through a few chapters and ta-da! Back on track.

The information in this book is well documented. I have read many books and watch many documentaries in the past years. I will be mentioning these books, authors and documentaries throughout the book so you can get them if you so desire. It is entirely up to you. I am only suggesting that you do. Not here to turn you into a religious freak or spiritual guide. Just here to help me first, remember. If it buzzes with you, great. There are quotes from all books that I have read; what resonates with me; some ah-ha moments I had; and there might even be some questions that never been answered but are just there to make me dream or meditate.

There has been and are still some very great teachers on this planet. Some come in some very peculiar fashion. Some people might be offended by them, but I always say to keep an open mind on all things. There is always something to learn.

If you feel you should continue reading, I need for you to not be judgemental about this book. Like I said, it's not for you but for me. If you are insulted by that phrase, well maybe you shouldn't continue reading, because there are some pretty divergent subjects and not everyone is ready to hear what I have to say. However, it does work for me and everyone should find a way to be grounded and at the same time part of the big Picture.

As you may know, I am not a prophet. I am only a very ordinary girl who just has found her balance in life and wants to share her story. As one of my best friends, Chris, once said: "Your story matters... "

So, good reading. I have put lots of space for you to write your own comments in this book. I find that all books I have read have never enough space to write your thoughts, spur of the moment ideas, and your insights. I always say that we need to read a book with the possibility that you are going to learn something or that it will move something inside of you. I sometime will read a sentence in a book and turn around and write three pages in my journal regarding that simple little sentence. If you find the urge to write something, go ahead. Make it your own book. Write some things that will make you feel good later on. We never know. Maybe reading this book will put you on your own quest of understanding. Maybe it will entice you to read more, learn more. This is one of the parts that we are here for: to learn more. Thus the reason we are always asking the question: "Why?"

And finally, be assured that **"You are blessed more than you have ever been told. You are loved more that you have ever been told. You are a wonderful unique being. Don't ever forget this".** Write it and place it somewhere that you will see it every day. Don't let your body tell you otherwise.

And now, turn the page, and dive into what you might want to call – after you read it all – some different way of looking into life that doesn't need that much effort.

"You are blessed more than you have ever been told. You are loved more that you have ever been told. You are a wonderful unique being. Don't ever forget this".

My own quote!

We are here to learn.

WHO IS CAROLE?

Well… It should be absolutely normal that if all of my chapters start with a question, I should title this one with yet another question. lol…

This is for me a very profound question. Because, like anybody being asked this question, we tend to think about what happened to us as being the definition of who we are, and we also tend to believe that it does define us. However, with all this time passed through reading and learning, I have finally have the outmost definition to "Who is Carole?": "an amazing being – or beam – of light that took her time to finally find herself".

If anyone reading this definition doesn't understand what I am trying to explain, the reading of this book will totally define this answer. AND it will also show you that you are also that amazing being – or beam – of light. Maybe you have already found yourself or maybe you need to find yourself, both individual fitting this description will enjoy reading this book.

But let's make one point clear right at the beginning… like the title states: "This book is not for you"…. It is written to help me go through life challenges.

Now, if you want to know more about what happened in the life of the being name Carole, you could say that she went through hell and back, a few times, like most people on this planet. But the thing is that I never stalled into hell. I always came out of it. Sometimes it took me a long time to get out of it. Some other times it seemed like it took me forever. So, this is why I wrote this book to help me get out of hell faster... lol.

I promised myself that I wouldn't get into the nitty gritty of Carole's life. However, sometimes it is good to point out a few things that happened in Carole's life so people can relate to her. Sort of saying: "Geez, she is just like me", or "OMG, that also happened to me", so that people can say to themselves: "If she can do it, so can I".

Carole is going to be 60 years old this coming November. She was born into a moderately financially at ease family. The oldest of the family, it seemed that her mother had decided that she was to be an example to the two other siblings, which Carole didn't really think it should be her vocation... lol.

In the summer of her 9th year, a very dramatic situation happened in her life where someone of her immediate entourage, a neighbour, molested her. This took the sparkle out of Carole's life. It took her a very long time to understand that it wasn't her fault and that situation wasn't what should define her as a being. She has regain her sparkle with the help of this book.

She lost some very important people in her past years, her grandmother and grandfather from her father's side of the family and of course her father, which was her best friend ever. She misses them a lot. However, she finally understood the meaning of life, which will be explaining in much more details in this book.

She also got married and that didn't work out great. And, also went through another relationship which didn't work out great either. But the most joyful events happened through those two relationships and that is the birth of a daughter in the first one, and the upbringing of a common law granddaughter in the second one: two most joyful blessings.

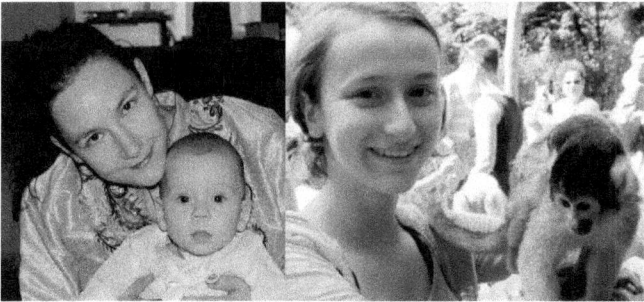

When she turned 47 year old, tired of asking the same questions over and over again, and never getting the answers, she decided to take a course in Natural Healing and became a Natural Health Practitioner. Since that time, she has been on a quest to help herself and other people that are also looking for answers, and always tries to answer in a way that is easiest to understand.

Carole had a very interesting life – many challenges – but asked if she would change something in it, and the answer would be: "No! Never in a million years." Because she has found the true meaning of life and its ways of enjoying it to the fullest.

With the help of this book, Carole has finally found Peace.

LOL... kind of enjoyed writing this little biography of "Moi". So, why not do the same? Let's see if you can write a few lines describing your life. Even if you feel that there is not a happy ending right now, read the book and then come back to your few lines written and maybe you will be able to rearrange a few lines and make it a happy ending!

Happy writing and good reading!

WHO IS (WRITE IN YOUR NAME
_____?)

_____

_____

_____

_____

_____

_____

_____

_____

_____

_____

_____

_____

_____

_____

_____

_____

_____

_____

_____

_____

_____

Chapter 1

WHY THE HECK AM I HERE FOR?

So really! Why are we here? What is our purpose here? Those questions kept resonating in my head and the more I would ask, the more I would get confused and depressed. Any of you out there has or had those same feelings? This chapter will deal more with the why and we'll investigate the "depressed" later in another chapter. However, I have always felt the need to know why. Why can't we get along? Why is the world in such a bad state? Why does she treat me that way? So, I have always been on a quest. I'll start around 2005 because I feel this is where I really truly started to be enlightened.

Here I am, out of a job, on Employment Insurance and nowhere to go, again. Feeling empty, not feeling useful, still searching what the heck I should do to make me feel good inside. A friend of mine suggested that I get evaluated, tested, to see what were my strengths, so that it would help me determine what I should do in life.

So here I go, to this special governmental office, to get tested. Well, that didn't really turned out like I hoped for, since the two strengths that came out strong were teaching and working in the health care profession. How did that turn out like this anyway? The lady that had given me the test started asking questions and soon to found out that I had some kind of incline towards natural health. Why not? Always wanted to know why I was sick and others weren't. Always wanted to know more about the human body. But don't put me in a situation where I would have to give a needle to someone. Just the thought of it makes me all dizzy.

Teaching? No way. Put me in a class full of kids that misbehave and I surely wouldn't last a week. However, I always enjoyed teaching adults that wanted to learn. When I was a District Manager for Avon, I really enjoyed the part where I would help them go through the six level of training, and see them evolve into a better person mentally and emotionally. So maybe this test wasn't that bad after all.

So, I finally found an institution that would allow me to learn online and started a one year training course as a Natural Health Practitioner.

The first two months were hell on earth. Here I am, 47 year old, trying to get something in that stubborn head of mine. I couldn't read a sentence without either looking in a Thesaurus or the medical dictionary, trying to understand what I was reading about. I then started to think that I had made a huge mistake and decided to talk about this to my teacher. She encouraged me by saying that I was on the right track, wasn't behind and said something to me that only resonated with me just a few months ago:

"Give some time for
your brain to adjust
with the changes".

So back to the books I went. This was fascinating! I then enjoyed each sentence as if it was a new world I was getting into. Still to this day I find the human body fascinating and full of miracles.

This course not only made me acquire more knowledge, but also saved my live. At that time, I was going the wrong path in dealing with my health and I was very sick. Maybe not sick enough for the regular doctors but nevertheless not in the right path. We'll talk more about healthy bodies in the coming chapters.

Still that little voice inside of me was tugging at my heart saying: "Why are you here, Carole? Who are you, really?" But little did I know I was going to start a new path just around the corner.

The year passed and I got my certificate. During that year, I got to know new people and I was introduced to Randy Gage[4]. If any of you like inspirational speakers, you will find Mr. Gage very different. Even though he tells you "Why you're dumb, sick and broke [5]" – the title of one of his books by the way – I enjoyed everything he has written and still follow his blog.

I also got to know lots of new people. I met this guy online who came from Trois-Rivières, Quebec. Even though I didn't meet him in person, we did chat every day for a while and exchanged ideas. One day, he told me that he had receive a DVD and since it was all in English and he was very French, he asked me for my address so he could send it to me.

So, it had been about three weeks, still haven't received it, I asked him if he had sent it. He answered positively. Meanwhile, I received an email from Randy Gage, telling me that I should be on the lookout next Monday for an extraordinary event that will change my life. I didn't make much of it at that time, but the next Monday before opening Randy's email, I received the DVD from my friend. It was called "The Secret [6]". Just holding it gave me my first sets of goosebumps. That was very weird for me at that time, but now I know that when it happens, something good will manifest just around the corner.

I went upstairs – my office was in the basement – and sat down to not only a DVD but a life changing event. The way the DVD starts was everything I could feel and live at that time. My life was in shambles, my dad – my best friend ever – had died, my job wasn't even working as it was planned. I was crying in the first few minutes of that movie. It changed my whole way of looking at everything. It's all about "**FEELING GOOD**".

It took me a while to understand that when you are asking yourself that question, "Why the heck am I here for?", at this point you need to start something new and exciting. That is what you are here for: finding things that are going to make you "**FEEL GOOD**".

I like this quote:

> "If you are not happy
> where you are, move!
> You are not a tree."

Learn to paint, learn to speak Spanish, or join a yoga class. You don't have money? Go for a walk, a swim in the ocean, meet new people. Find something or someone that will make you "**FEEL GOOD**". These are the words that Rhonda Byrne[7] – author of "The Secret" – wrote in the sand at the end of the movie. Here is the "catch 22": As your thoughts wonder, you tend to forget to "**FEEL GOOD**". Almost like the wave of the ocean tend to erase that "**FEEL GOOD**" scripture in the sand. So you need to remind yourself often, or rewrite the "**FEEL GOOD**" in the sand.

"**FEEL GOOD**" would be your second statement that you should plaster your house, car and even office at work with. So that you do not forget!

So, what are we here for? To "**FEEL GOOD**".

Took me almost 12 years to understand that affirmations do work. I finally decided to write this book because I need to remind me of this every time I felt down. Later in the book I will explain why we tend to forget. It is imperative that you remind yourself over and over again.

The next step that I needed to understand was about those goosebumps. Why was it that I had those goosebumps just by holding a book, a DVD or just passing by a shelf full of books?

Oh! And by the way! Randy's email was just one of his ways to get us excited or curious about his next move. Still does it in all kinds of different ways... lol.

"FEEL GOOD"

From the movie "The Secret"

NOTES

Chapter 2

IS THERE A GOD?

A lot of my friend are going to say: "What is she getting into? For sure there is a God!!!" And I will answer: "Yes, there is a God, but maybe not necessarily the God you are thinking about". Many people think that God is a person, It is not. God is a collectiveness of all the energy there is in the Universe. There I said it.

Call it God, Universe, Source, or Spirit, it is all the same thing. What is important here is to know that we are part of something that is way bigger than ourselves. You see, there is the Universe, and in the Universe there are the galaxies, and then the planets, and on our planet there are human beings, and our body includes organs that are made out of cells, and the cells are made with molecules, and the molecules are then made with atoms and in the atoms is pure energy. Any form that we see, and don't see, is made of pure energy.

Now, what is energy? This is a bit more complicated. My dad was an electrician. He thought me a few things about energy. However, I truly didn't understand it at that time. But, I knew that when I flipped the switch, there was energy going to bulb and it would light it up. For me or you to know the what's and how's the energy is created and goes through the wire and directly to the bulb is irrelevant here, because this is something that everybody depends on and if we don't have electricity, we call someone else and they take care of it.

But what about the energy that flows through our body? Is it the same? Yes it is. They are the same atoms that are in that form which is our body. I don't know if any of you ever watched the movie "The Matrix"[8], but when Neo finally becomes what Morpheus was wishing for, Neo sees only energy that flows from the forms. That could be a very good example to explain what is the energy flowing from form and into form.

Our body is made of those same atoms. We are made of that same energy. There is something that does regulate it, but we'll talk about this later on. But for now, what is important is that we know about this energy and that we are intricately all connected through that same energy.

I like the way James Arthur Ray[9] defines what energy is in the movie "The Secret".

> *Most people define themselves by this finite body, but you're not a finite body. Even under a microscope you're an energy field. What we know about energy is this: You go to a quantum physicist and you say, "What created the world?" And he or she will say, "Energy." Well, describe energy. "OK, it can never be created or destroyed, it always was, always has been, everything that ever existed always exists, it's moving into form, through form and out of form."*

You go to a theologian and ask the same question, "What created the Universe?" And he or she will say, "God." OK, describe God. "Always was always has been, never can be created or destroyed, all that ever was, always will be, always moving into form, through form and out of form." You see, it's the same description, just different terminology.

So if you think you're this "meat suit" running around, think again. You're a spiritual being! **You're an energy field, operating in a larger energy field.**

So, for some it is a bit far fetch, but we are all energy. Even a though is energy, but again, we'll go through that later in the book.

I believe in God. I don't believe that we need to go to University and have a degree to know about God. I don't believe that we need to pay to get that knowledge, because it is right inside of us already. We just need to understand it, believe it, and accept it.

Some people will turn away from or turn to God when something bad or good happens in their lives. What happened was destined. It is hard to accept but everything that happens, has to happen. It's the flow of energy that brews with what is going on. It is the energy that is already set to happen.

For example: you do not catch a cold because you didn't put on your hat. You catch a cold because your immune system is down, or maybe because of the glass of orange juice that you didn't take with your breakfast this morning. Thus, putting your immune system out of the nutrients it needed. Everything goes with the law of cause and effect, the law of attraction.

Dr. Joe Vitale[10], again in the movie "The Secret", explains:

> *Everything that surrounds you right now in your life, including the things you're complaining about, you've attracted. Now I know at first blush that's going to be something that you hate to hear. You're going to immediately say, "I didn't attract the car accident. I didn't attract this particular client who gives me a hard time. I didn't particularly attract the debt." And I'm here to be a little bit in your face and to say, yes you did attract it. This is one of the hardest concepts to get, but once you've accepted it, it's **life transforming**.*

True indeed. Very life transforming. To accept what is, will change your entire perception of life.

So, energy is there to manipulate. What do you want it to do for you? How do you do it? By simple thought... very hard to understand but it will be explain in detail through the book.

What you need to understand at this point is that **we are part of something way bigger that you can imagine**. Our life doesn't revolve around just ourselves. It is part of everyone and everything surrounding us.

Everyone go back to learn from prophets (Jesus, Buddha, etc.) that lived before us. They understood that concept. They knew how to work with It. However, some don't necessarily understand the teachings and writings and will distort the true meaning of it so that they can benefit themselves. Unfortunately, they are not necessarily at the same level of understand and this is something that we need to accept. Those people are just not at the same stage as we are. They need to learn at their own pace. To accept and allow this is a great beginning in the search of your true self. When you finally understand how everything works, it is a liberating feeling.

We are all part of a whole. Anything that divides us, is not the solution. The first step to understand this better would be not to be part, if need be, of a group that is against something. If you are against war, be pro-peace. If you are against abortion, be pro-life. The best is to **let it be**, like the song says. The only part of you that is not understand this, and doesn't want to accept what is the opposite of your thinking, is your ego. We'll have some great solutions to how to tame that beast later on.

About the goosebumps... since energy flows through all forms, this means that any intent also has energy. So, a book is made of energy. Who wrote that book is made of energy. His or her thoughts are energy. So, if by passing by something or someone that gives you goosebumps, it means that you are directly align with that specific energy field that this something or someone is creating, and is attracting you. Don't miss out! Explore the event. If something or someone makes you turn around, you better find out the why of this action. As Dr. Vitale mentioned:

> "Everything that surrounds you right now in your life … you've attracted."

One thing that I am not going to avoid talking about, or should I say not make the same mistake that the movie "The Secret" did, is to hide the true character of Esther Hicks in the first "Secret" movie that was made. Yes, there were two movies. In the first take, Esther Hicks was part of it. In the second movie, they took her out or should I say, she removed herself. I'll let you google the reason why.

When I first watched the movie – many times, lol – one of the characters in the movie was Esther Hicks, from the Teaching of Abraham. What she was talking about made a lot of sense. For some reason at that time, I didn't googled her. I was more interested in Joe Dispenza's work, which I learned from the movie "What the bleep do we know?"[11] I will talk more about these findings later on in this book.

Now, how I was introduced to Esther Hicks brought loads of goosebumps. I have a friend that shared many of my thoughts and feelings, and one day I was visiting her and we started talking about the movie "The Secret". For some reason – and it was meant to be – we started talking about the individual characters in the movie. When I mentioned Esther Hicks, she was a bit confused because to her knowledge there were no one by that name that she remembered in the movie. However, she had greater knowledge about her work than I did.

She had a copy of the movie and we put it on, and as we were viewing it, I kept saying: "Ok, this is the part that she comes in", and it wouldn't happen. So, for a while I felt very confused and wondered why I would have received a copy of a DVD that is not the same as the one that my friend had. It was meant to be.

So, here goes. Esther Hicks is a medium. There, I said it. Abraham is an entity, a group or collectiveness that speaks through Esther Hicks. Weird? Try to picture my face when I was told that... lol. I had already encountered this concept but never really took it seriously. I have had a medium told me a lot of things when I was about 25 years old. Most of what he had told me came true, but never really put all the pieces together, until my new journey had started with the movie "The Secret".

So, as of that day, I started to watch, listen and read everything about the Teaching of Abraham. Made a lot of sense to me. I investigated more on this concept. I even returned to see another medium to learn more. That was a turning point in my life. This is where I learned about our true powers, the limitations that we give us, and what amazing being we truly are. All will be captured in this book.

So, if you haven't freaked out already, I invite you to continue reading.

"You're an energy field, operating in a larger energy field."

James Arthur Ray

NOTES

Chapter 3

WHY ARE PEOPLE SO MEAN?

I need to constantly reread this chapter, because I tend to get into situation where people will take advantage of me. Now, I know that I need to work on this one because I just made an affirmation and placed it in the Universe, thus this could happen to me just because I thought about it. Complicated? We'll get into the more complicated later on. However, this book that I am writing is to give me the "how to not" get into those situations or to remove me from those situations without harm done.

There is a big difference between hurt and harm. Hurt means that it is hurting me at this moment. It is painful, but it can be made well with care. Harm is a little bit deeper. The harm can last for a very long time if let be. The worst harm that you can experience is the hurt that someone has done to you mentally and you feel the harm every time that you think about it, every time you see that person, and every time a similar situation happens.

Harm is what makes your mind go: "I don't want to go there anymore". Hurt is making your mind go: "Be careful next time not to do the same thing to hurt yourself": Wear protective glasses, gloves or an apron.

Harm is caused by reoccurring thoughts of the same scenario going on and on in your mind.

To break free from this, needs forgiveness. Some people are going to say: "I am not ever going to forgive that person. She is a vicious and unscrupulous person that only thinks about herself and she doesn't deserve that I forgive her." However, the forgiveness doesn't necessarily mean that it needs to be towards that person but should be pointed towards you for allowing that person to have hurt you in the first place. It is only harm when the feeling persists.

You can, if you want to, talk to that person and let her know that she has indeed hurt you. But sometimes, this can be more harmful because that person may not believe that she has hurt you and will even aggravate the situation by telling you that you are a silly person to believe such a thing. That person can also really don't care about what you have to say. So, if a person continuously hurts you, the best is to forgive yourself for allowing something like this to happen to you and move on. Distance yourself of that person if need be.

I always say, find people of same liking. Don't try to change people or the world. Work on yourself and the rest will follow. There are over seven billion people on this planet. There are some good and some bad. Choose wisely.

Another person that I really enjoyed reading and

listening to is Jim Rohn[12]. Unfortunately, he left is physical body but his legacy stays. He used to say that in your entire life on earth you will only encounter about ten mean people. However, they do move around a lot, and you might bump into them more often than you want to, during the span of your lifetime ... lol.

I have had many experiences with people taking advantage of my giving spirit. Giving makes me happy and makes me "**FEEL GOOD**" inside. What I need to be careful with is to whom I am giving, and make sure that the people that I am giving to are no leaches – people that only stick around to pick up every bread crumb. It might be a harsh definition, and I know that I shouldn't be judging, however I need for you – and also I, because I am writing this book for my future – to get a clear picture.

We also need to know about the law of opposite. **There is white and black**. Darkness and light, and there will always be mean people and good people. Accept and move on. The only reason why there is a law of opposite, is for us to know the difference. You don't need to stay in a bad situation. You can create a new situation any time. It will not be done in a day. It might take a long time, but it is doable. You have to have faith, hope, and

love yourself more every day, and of course a plan that works, like this book for me.

Also, you need to understand that those mean people might be going through something right now that they do not understand themselves. Like I said before, everyone learns at his or her own pace. When you know about this, you can tell yourself that he or she is not where you are at, and let them be. Let them figure out what is wrong in their own picture. Don't be the Joan of Arc and try to fix everyone's problems. You have your own problems still to work on. This is not called selfishness. It is fixing you before trying to help others fix themselves.

In the Bible it says to "turn the other cheek". It doesn't mean that you need to let everyone walk over you. There is another part of the bible that says to "shake the dust off your feet and move on". I like that one better.

I don't know if you ever had a chance to watch a group of ducks swim peacefully on a lake. It is so serine, so beautiful. All of a sudden, for no apparent reason, two ducks will face each other and start honking at each other and get a bit physical as if one duck is saying to the other: "You are in my space, move on". Right after the interaction, both ducks will turn away from each other and just flap their wings vigorously as if they are releasing the negative energy which just happened. We need to be more like these ducks.

Flap your wings or dust your feet off. Two nice analogies that I cherish.

Nature is the best teacher. You can learn a lot just by watching your pet cat or dog. It gives you joy just by pathing them. They are always happy to see you. They hold no grudge. They are the best pals. However, we live in a society of very different people and we need to find a way to belong. To finally get to be okay with this, I needed to take some distance from everyone for a while and go very deep inside of myself and learn to get closer to people very slowly. I've seen myself sometimes taking one step at a time and other times taking a few steps back. The secret is to go at your own pace, and not at someone else's suggestions. It is your life and you should be able to be the master of it.

Besides the goosebumps, there is another phenomenon that I have learned to trust. Some call it the gut feeling.

If ever I get this reverse feeling in my solar plexus, I become like a cat that needs to re-examine the next few steps it had anticipated to take, however, it is now recalculating its moves.

We also need to understand that there are a lot of hurting units out there. And when someone is hurt, they also do hurtful things. I know that when I was hurt, I have done things that didn't really help other people in my surroundings. With age we tend to become wiser and see patterns. This wisdom comes with the years of being into similar situations, I guess.

So, the next time you have someone being mean to you, just read these pages. It will definitively make you feel better. It's all about "**FEELING GOOD**". Remember?

NOTES

Chapter 4

WHO SHOULD I LISTEN TO?

When you are young, we are told to listen to our parents. In school, we need to listen to the teacher. At work, it is definitively going to be the boss. But what do they mean to listen to the voice of reasoning? In the Bible, God would pop up in the scenario as a burning bush. Has men been so not able to decide by himself, or did he always needed to have something or someone else to tell him what to do?

I have listened to many people. As of today, none of those suggestions have made me a better person. I have maybe made those people satisfied in their quest of making Carole be their puppet, but none of their suggestions have made me proud, satisfied, achieved, or rich. But every time that I was told something by someone else, there has been that little tug at my heart. A feint voice inside saying: "I wouldn't do that if I were you". We could consider that the voice of reasoning.

It comes to you when you are at most not truly feeling it. You tell yourself later: "Ah, shucks! I should have done this – or not." This is, what is called by many now, your guiding system.

Remember in a previous chapter I explain about

energy? Well, we are an energy field within another energy field. The inner energy field, which is connected to the outer energy field – Source – is telling or showing you what to do or not to do. Now, I am not talking about the ego, because the ego will make you do things that you really shouldn't do. So, how do we know if it is our true self or our ego?

Very easy! The ego will always only think about the one, not the self but the one. The one is the part that believes in possessions, accumulations, selfishness, not giving, and anything that is about riches. Something like the "precious". The self or the inner self – the inner energy field – thinks always about the whole, others, and community.

This might take some work to understand, but the next time that you are in a circumstance that you need to make a decision, ask yourself: "Will this benefit only me, or by doing so will I contribute to the collectiveness?"

Now, let's be realistic here too. When it comes to your health, it is very important that you choose to better your health. Don't believe that God is keeping you ill for a purpose. In no way God, the Universe, or Source would want to keep you ill as an example to others. There is enough illness in this world that we can see the difference between ill and healthy. Don't either believe that you are not worthy. You are more than worthy. When you think these thoughts, you are in a state where the body has taken over your mind and you need to shake yourself out of this misery. We will be talking more about this state soon.

For a long time I have been in a depressive mood. Not being able to get out of it. I had to reprogram my mind, my body and find my true self to help me with this. Speaking to yourself is not madness... lol. If there is an energy field within another energy field, yes I talk to myself. Sometimes it may even feel that there are 3 people in here: Your divine self, consciousness and sub-consciousness. We'll talk more about that later on too.

So, who do you listen too? Always listen to yourself first. You are the one that has to deal with what is going to be done, so it is crucial that you have a say into what need to be done. It is not called selfishness, it is called self-awareness. It's being present, in the moment. It is not being untrustworthy. It is helping you be there, really grasping what is going on.

Mind you that there are people out there that you need to be careful with. They will make you do anything in their power so they can accumulate the riches. Some will put you in a position that they don't want to be in, and when they see that you prosper and surpass their egotistical rank, then they will make you look bad or use their rank to lower you back to what they believe you should be so that they can stay number one in their egotistical mind. Promotions do that to a lot of people. They believe that they are better than you and they will do everything they can to keep it that way, unfortunately.

But you should never feel lower than anyone on this planet. You are worthy. You are here for a reason and the first reason is .... "**FEELING GOOD**"! And the first person that you should be listening to is yourself, no exception.

Some might say that you should be listening to God first. God is within. We are made in the image of God. God is the energy field which all energy fields are made of, including yourself. Our inner energy field is part of God. So who do you listen to? In a sense, we are listening to God when we listen to our true self, our inner energy field, or our guiding system. And, that guidance system will never put you in a situation that is not appropriate, self-destructive, and in any emotionally negative circumstances. Your inner guidance wants you to thrive, be happy, and flourish. If you egotistically accept to do something that your inner guiding system didn't agree with, you are not going to be punished but will have to deal with any consequences that might emerge. God doesn't punish, like a lot of people tend to believe. It allows.

We are here to learn. When a child learns to walk, he falls down and gets back up again. Same for adults. We fall and we learn to get back on our feet, over and over again.

So, we are here to "**FEEL GOOD**" and to learn... which brings us to our next chapter.

NOTES

Chapter 5

WHAT TRULY DRIVES US?

I might be a bit offensive to some in this chapter. Many will just close the book and toss it away to maybe open it again later on in life... lol – or maybe never. But here goes...

We are spiritual being, yes. But that "meat suit" that we have, has other ideas and the first idea it has, is to pro-create. Nothing wrong with this. But the word sex to some people might be something that they do not want to hear, to others is "please give me more". Everything that is form needs to be replaced after their expiry date, which date we do not know about. So to replace this beautiful specie that we are, we need to do the horizontal mambo at some point in time... lol.

So in a certain way, sex drives us to procreate.

But when I ask the question: "What truly drives us?", I was more emphasizing on the "us" as a community than the egotistical "us". So the "meat suit" need to procreate, but our inner self doesn't, because it never dies, it is always there and always will be. It just moves on to maybe a different "meat suit" – or should I say another energy field so that I don't sound too vulgar... lol.

What drives the inner field? We are here to experience

new experiences. Learn new things that makes us "**FEEL GOOD**". Our outer energy field, the one that comprises our mind which includes our sub-conscious, can limit us sometimes because of what was taught in this life or previous lives, brought to us through means of learning from the past or experiences.

Let me explain... if you were told as a young child that if you do not eat your carrots, you will have bad eye site, that auto-suggestion may affect unintentionally your sight. More and more scientific proof that suggestions or affirmations lined up with an intent can change your behavioral pattern and even your physical appearance or growth.

Like I was saying in a previous chapter, Dr. Joe Dispenza was my first interest after I watched the movie "The Secret". I got into the movie "What the bleep do we know" and of course Dr. Joe Dispenza. He spoke scientifically about the changes that occurs in our body, not the woohoo way – has some would really like to call it.

The movie "What the bleep do we know", was definitively for me going deeper into the rabbit hole.

The Natural Health Practitioner course gave me a good overview of how the body works, but to really understand what makes the body work the way it does work, Dr. Dispenza took me through the realm of the nervous system and what makes the nervous system work from outside of our body.

So, like I mentioned before. There is the Universe, then there is the galaxy, then the planet, then the human being, then the organs, then the cells, then the molecules, then the atoms and then energy. So that latter energy is in another energy field that is in another energy field that is in another energy field that is in another energy field... do you get the picture? We are all connected... So, in the body field are all those other energy fields (organs, cells, molecules, atoms) and there is also us. When we leave, there is still energy that needs to – excuse my expression – return the "meat suit" to another form – dirt. From dust we came, to dust we return. But the true self is eternal.

When we accept that concept, it is very liberating. I have accepted that one day, my "meat form" will dissolve but my eternal being will live on. Makes me look at life and living a very different way. I do not worry about dying any more. Anyway, worries are something else that I have no more. Why worry about something that might not happen? All that worrying will only give you health problems, which we will be discussed soon.

Let's go back to the God concept ... There are some groups on this planet that want you to believe that if you do not believe in God, and other group go as far as if you do not believe in the Son of God, you will not go to heaven – meaning that your soul will perish in hell. You are already part of God, the Universe, the Source, or Being. These groups are dividing us. Yes there is what we call sides: good or bad, white and black, etc. But when it comes to energy, we are all in the same boat. However, we need to accept that they are not at the same level as we are, they are learning at their own pace and their way of looking at things is okay for them. You move to your own beat of the drum and you let others find their own way. If we start saying that they are wrong and we are right, it only brings division. We need to let them be. Their right is right for them, and we move on.

What is important here, is to not get into other people's power trips. Also, I am not here to change your world. I am just helping myself achieve my own greatness and at the same time letting you know how I can achieve it. I am not saying that they are wrong in thinking what they are thinking. But they are very wrong in instilling fear in people so that these people follow their beliefs. People should have the right to think what they want.

So we are here to procreate, we are here to live different experiences, we are here to learn about our true self, and we are here to "**FEEL GOOD**".

The next part of the book is all about how our body works and I truly believe that this part should be taught in school at a very young age.

Ladies and gentlemen, let's dive into what is called the most marvelous machine ever created... the human body.

NOTES

Chapter 6

AND, WHAT PART DOES THE BODY HAS TO DO IN THIS?

Normally, we should start with the most important part and finish with the least important: energy, atoms, molecules, cells, organs and then body. However, in our society the energy in the body is not well understood.

The body should be the puppet. But, it can easily become the puppeteer, if let be.

What is about to be introduced to you, if this is the first time you ever had a chance to really look into the body, should be taught to our children as soon as possible. For some reason, through the years, the body has been misunderstood by young children. Take away the skin, and you have a scary skeleton. How can you take care of your body, if you don't even know how it works or if it scares you?

Within the energy field called the body are many other energy fields. We will start with the systems:

1. Integumentary System: Skin, hair and nails

2. Structural System: bones

3. Muscular System

4. Nervous System

5. Endocrine System - Hormonal

6. Cardiovascular System

7. Lymphatic and immune System

8. Respiratory System

9. Digestive System

10. Urinary System

11. Reproductive System: which are two very distinctive systems both on woman and man

For the sake of keeping this book to a minimal, I will only emphasize on the Nervous system. However, every system are very intricately in need of each other. Remember, they are energy fields within energy fields. Some systems have energy fields within that specific energy field. Like the digestive system, there is the stomach, the liver, and the intestines that are by themselves energy fields. And, to emphasize what I have said about needing other systems, it also needs the participation of the pancreas, which is also part of the Endocrine system. Everything needs everything to work in perfect harmony. However, it is not always known by many of us and we don't really know what is going on in our own body.

At some point in time, some body parts are taken out. To give you some example of that, I could very well quote my own life. At age 16, they took my tonsils out. At age 40, the uterus and one ovary. At age 52, my gallbladder.

At age 16, I knew nothing about the human body. Tonsils are an intricate part of the Immune System. Take them out, and then your Immune System needs to find other ways to compensate, it will work harder. This will put strain on other part of the body and then you don't have a harmonized body.

At age 40, still didn't have any clue how the body worked and how important my uterus was to my hormonal balances. Again, the body needs specific hormones and it will produce them elsewhere. However, to speak of a certain hormone, like progesterone, they can also be produced by the adrenal glands situated on top of the kidneys which also help the body control blood sugar, burn protein and fat, react to stressors like a major illness or injury, and regulate blood pressure. Stress this organ and then you have other health problems that come about. It is all intricately connected. Every cell needs every cell. Every organ needs every organ. Every system needs every system. Every human needs every human. Doesn't it make you wonder why our planet is so much in turmoil?

At age 52, I knew better. However, I was so much in pain that I couldn't say no to the operation. What had triggered the attack was a massive emotional stress. The night before my attack, I had a very concerning telephone call and I was very sad for about 24 hours, crying, sobbing. The action of me deeply sobbing, dislodged tiny stones off my gallbladder and accumulated in the conduit between the gallbladder and liver, where the bile normally accumulates. The stones blocked the bile, and there was no other way of looking at it but to operate, from the point of view of a doctor.

When in deep pain, either emotional or structural pain, we have difficulty to make sense or to follow through what is logical. Confusion settles in when we are bombarded by suggestions from people around us. This is where you need to have time to yourself and coach yourself into a meditative state to have a clearer picture of what is going on and how your solar plexus (gut feeling) is feeling with what you are dealing with and the action you are taking regarding this dilemma.

Hope this helped you understand a little more about why everything is so important and why we should be more attentive to our body.

Then we will be studying the cell. Many different cells in the body and each has its own thing to do to make sure that each system is nourished with the proper nutrients. Each cell is its own individual entity, its own energy field. However, it needs others to survive. The same as ourselves in this world again. Makes you wonder sometimes the association there is with the functions of our body and what is going on in this world. I truly believe if we would understand more how our body works that we would be more careful how we treat our neighbors.

After looking at the cell, we'll get into the nitty gritty of the molecules and the atoms. Very briefly again since there are tons of books that can go into those subjects. This book is only to make me remember what I need to know to get back on track, right?

Then we will go deeper into the rabbit hole, where most men have never been before, and I assure you it is not the final frontier.

So, let's begin...

The body, as a whole, is built with trillions of cells (way much more cells in our body than there are people on this planet). What is so amazing is that it all started with two different cells that collided, attracted to each other chemically.

The body needs – to survive – the four elements: sun, air, water and of course earth. (see blog at: www. cb-consulting.ca/facts-about-water/?lang=en) All our nutrients that our body consumes depend of these four elements. Everything comes from the earth: Our minerals – which feed the plants, which feeds the beef that we consume; our vitamins – that are manufactured by the plants. Everything comes from the earth, which is showered by the rain, kissed by the sun and feathered by the breeze the air has to offer. We have become a society of people that are too busy to give thanks for those elements that are keeping our body alive.

Key point: vitamin D and K are both produced by our body. Vitamin D is produced with the help of the sun and Vitamin K is produced in our intestinal tracts. Anyone that is deficient in Vitamin D should be in the sun at least 10 minutes every second day and for those that have Vitamin K deficiency, most of the time it is also related with a bowel dysfunction. Fix the problem and the deficiency goes away. There are some supplement that you can take, but they are chemicals, man-made. It is okay to take it for a period of time, until the problem is rectified. But the best vitamin D and K are the one that your body can produce by itself. For other facts about vitamins, visit:

www.cb-consulting.ca/facts-about-vitamins/?lang=en

One element that the body is bombarded with, and is not necessarily needed, are negative emotions. Not controlled, our emotions can do real damage to our body. They cause a chain reaction in the body that is very hard to reverse. Only knowledge of such damage can set you free. We will discuss this in depth in a later chapter.

Following, is a condensed descriptive definition of each of the systems found in our body.

1. Integumentary System – Skin, hair and nails:
    a. Is the outer shell of the body
    b. Protects deeper tissues from lesions
    c. Synthetizes Vitamin D

    d. Contains receptors for pain and pressure, etc., and sebaceous and sweat glands

2. Structural System: bones

    a. Support and protect organs

    b. Constitute a structure where the muscles produce movement

    c. Produce blood cells in the bone marrow

    d. Is also a mineral reserve

3. Muscular System

    a. Responsible for the manipulation of objects in the environment, locomotion, facial expression

    b. Maintains posture

    c. Produces heat

4. Nervous System

    a. Perceives stimuli

    b. Analyses information and instantly responds to intern and extern changes by activating the proper glands and muscles

5. Endocrine System - Hormonal

    a. Secrets hormones, regulating process like growth, reproduction and the cell's need for nutriments (metabolic process)

6. Cardiovascular System

    a. Transport the blood that contains oxygen, carbon dioxide, nutrients, hormones, and waste, etc.

    b. The heart circulates the blood, working like a pump

7. Lymphatic and immune System

    a. Gather liquids that escape from cardiovascular system and reroute it back to the same system

    b. Eliminates the waste from the lymphatic vessels with the help of the lymph nodes.

    c. Contains white blood cells which plays a crucial role in immunity, by attacking foreign substances in the organism.

8. Respiratory System

    a. Brings oxygen to the blood and rids the carbon dioxide – this exchange is made through the lungs.

9. Digestive System

    a. Breaks down the food to absorbable nutrients so that they can be distributed to the cells through the blood.

    b. The non-digested substances are rejected as stool

    c. See blog at: www.cb-consulting.ca/digestion/?lang=en

10. Urinary System

    a. Eliminate waste of nitrogenous composition

    b. Regulates fluids, electrolytes and blood's **pH balance** (very important to the survival of the body). See blog at <u>www.cb-consulting.ca/facts-about-acid-base-a-dynamic-balance/?lang=en</u>

11. Reproductive System: which are 2 very distinctive systems on woman and man

    a. Assures reproduction.

    b. Testicles produces sperm and the male sexual hormone, testosterone

    c. The male conduit and glandes allows proper transportation of the sperm into the vagina, which is also the birthing canal.

    d. Ovaries produces the ovum and the female hormones, progesterone and oestrogen.

    e. The uterus is the development space of the foetus.

    f. Breasts produces milk to nourish infant.

For other very informative details about the systems, please view:

<u>http://cb-consulting.ca/a-three-part-eye-opening-</u>

informative-blog-regarding-your-health-part-1/?lang=en

http://cb-consulting.ca/a-three-part-eye-opening-informative-blog-regarding-your-health-part-2/?lang=en

http://cb-consulting.ca/a-three-part-eye-opening-informative-blog-regarding-your-health-part-3/?lang=en

After looking at the body as a whole and its respective systems, like mentioned here and there, each system has different organs with different functions. When there is turmoil in one system, most of the energy will be placed into it, not giving attention to the other system. Then you have a body that is not only having one problem at one place but the whole is affected.

To briefly give you an example... If, for the sake of just making a point, you have issues with your blood sugar being high, it might mean that your pancreas is not producing enough insulin. Too much insulin in the blood will mean that your kidneys will be working harder. It might also mean that your cells are not taking in the sugar. They might be busy with some other issues, like being bombarded with peptides created by the hypothalamus and the pineal glands.

Each organ has a duty and if that duty is slowed down or stopped, the rest of the body will suffer.

And then we have the cells. Each cell also has different

functions. We have the nerve cells which collect information and govern the organism's functions. Muscle cells produce a mechanical action to move body parts. Red blood cells transports oxygen and nutrients throughout the body and white blood cells are part of our immune system. However, the main purpose of all cells, but the red and white blood cells, are to produce proteins. The body is a protein producing machine.

Enzymes are proteins. Hormones are proteins. Peptides are proteins. Each protein has a specific duty. Each cell needs different proteins to be able to function properly. If for any reason the production of a specific protein is reduced or halted, then we have potential threats to the body. Doctors call them diseases. What need to be done in this matter is finding the reason why the production has diminished or stopped. It can be temporarily replaced with a similar man-made chemical product until the reason is found and fixed. But the key word here is **temporarily**. No man-made substance should be a permanent solution. Of course, there are some exceptions. However, any problems taken care of at the source, at the beginning, would not necessitate the removal of organs or other body parts.

The cell is the smallest individual living part of our body besides some bacteria that can be good for the whole organism or some bad. Molecules are group of atoms bonded together and representing the smallest fundamental unit of a chemical compound that can take part in a chemical reaction. And then an atom is by itself the smallest particle of an element than can exist either alone or in combination.

To nourish the cell, we need oxygen and glucose. Glucose will be taken from the food we eat. The molecule of glucose is six part carbon, plus twelve part hydrogen, and six part oxygen. Don't ask me how this happened, or how it was knitted together. Never understood it, not interested in learning how it happened. I take the word from people that have studied in this field. Carbon, hydrogen and oxygen are called elements. Depending of what we are looking at, it is composed of different quantities of elements grouped together. Don't worry, I won't stay long on this subject. We just need to get to the part where there is energy so that we have finally got to the part that is the most important.

The atom is comprised of a nucleus – in the middle of course – and then depending what element we are talking about, this nucleus will have a specific number of protons and neutrons, and of course electrons moving around the nucleus. It is said that if the nucleus of an atom could be identified as being a basketball, its electrons, neutrons and protons would be flying somewhat around the nucleus as far as the length of a football field. Lots of empty space we would say... It is also said that if we could take all the nucleus of every atom on the planet, it would only be the size of a pea. Small enough for you?

Where the energy comes from is that the nucleus has a positive charge and the electrons have a negative charge, thus giving you electricity – energy. If you would like to have some kind of crash course on this, I suggest that you view the movie "What the bleep do we know". It is nicely explained.

Every single form is buzzing with the same energy. Nothing or no one is made different. The chair beside you is made with these same atoms. These atoms – that energy – is buzzing in every single human, plant, bird, and animal – we are made of energy.

So what governs that energy? The highest of energy: some call it God! This energy needs some kind of intelligence to behave, act the way it is supposed to. We – speaking of the form – are not the puppeteer. Anything related to flesh is not the boss of me – my true self.

So here's a question … who started all this? Had to be of extreme intelligence to create all this. Remember, for something to exist it needs to be created first.

A few questions to consider before we go any further, who or what controls us? Have you ever considered this? Do you believe, as a whole, the body has only one master, yourself? Who is "yourself", really? Is the brain or the mind in charge? Where is the mind in the body?

Can you see the mind? If the mind is in charge, how can you say: "I am losing my mind"? Who is "I" and what is the "mind"? Could the body be sometimes in control? Even Jesus mentioned a few times in the Bible about the flesh being in control. Only intelligence can be in control, don't you think? Where does the intelligence come from? The body – the cells – the brain/mind or our inner self? Can there be more than one entity in control of our own body?

Let's investigate this.

NOTES

Chapter 7

WHAT IS THE MIND?

It took me a long time before I understood this word in its entirety. When I finally learned that the mind is not a body part, it was the beginning of a long quest and which to date I am still on.

Since the word mind is associated with intelligence, lots of people, including myself, believed that the mind was part of the brain.

Intelligence: (1) The ability to learn or understand or to deal with new or trying situations – the skilled use of reason. (2) The ability to apply knowledge to manipulate one's environment or to think abstractly as measured by objective criteria (such as tests).

Mind: (1) The element of a person that enables them to be aware of the world and their experiences, to think, and to feel; the faculty of consciousness and thought. (2) A person's intellect.

Brain: (1) an organ of soft nervous tissue contained in the skull of vertebrates, functioning as the coordinating center of sensation and intellectual and nervous activity. (2) Intellectual capacity.

Thought: (1) an idea or opinion produced by thinking or occurring suddenly in the mind. (2) The action or process of thinking.

This is what I need to put down on paper, for me to read as often as it needs be. For me this part of the book is my reminder that we are very complex beings.

The brain, by itself – its anatomic values – is an organ: flesh. The nervous system is the first to be created in the embryonic stage of the foetus. If you think about yourself as being the true master puppeteer, then where were you in this initial stage of development? This is where we can capture the essence of the soul at work, our true self.

The person that we call ourselves is developed later, through experiences. But at the embryonic stage, we can capture the essence of God, the Universe, or Source – call it what you want. Our soul is working with God to create a new life.

From now on, I'll be quoting many passages I have read in books. These passages remind me of how complex we are.

Thinking – that occurs in the mind – is what makes us human. Thinking can come from your own egotistical mind or can also come from your conscience. The conscience is what is truly connected to the Source. For purpose of being on the same line, from now on I will also refer to God and Universe as being Source. For me it is a Source of everything. Your conscience cannot be egotistical.

Consciousness: is the state or quality of awareness,

or, of being aware of an external object or something within oneself.

Subconsciousness: *is the part of your mind which operates without your awareness and over which you do not have active control... (Really? What if we do have control?)*

Conscience is that little voice inside that either tells you to do it or not to do it. Some call it your gut feeling. To determine if it is your conscience or either your ego speaking to you, you only need to determine if the act that you are about to follow through is directly lined up to your own needs and feelings or if it is directed to humanity. True, buying that nice necklace makes you feel good, but it is not everlasting. It is an egotistical choice. But then you say: "Well I need sometimes to do something nice for myself". Yes, true! But this is where we make the division into the masses of who really cares about others and who cares only about themselves.

There is nothing wrong about being rich. More money means more to help others. If you have the power to make more money, by all means do it. However, if it is an egotistical power of just having more, then you are not in the right track.

Talking about tracks, I just went off it a bit... My mind was wondering into the abyss... lol.

Before we go any further, I need to quote from Dr. Joe Dispenza's book, "Evolve your brain" (pages 73 – 75).

*Our brain primarily consists of nerve cells called neurons. In many ways, neurons are the most specialized cells and the most sensitive type of tissue of all biological systems. They process information and pass it on to other neurons, thus initiating specific actions in other parts or our brain and body. Most significantly, **neurons are the only cells in the body that communicate directly with one another**; they send messages back and forth in the form of electrochemical signals or impulses.*

Not only are neurons the most significant cells that make up the brain, they also are the most fundamental component of our nervous system: the intricate network of structures, consisting of the brain, spinal cord, and nerves, that controls and coordinates all the functions of our bodies. The unique way that nerve cells communicate is what makes the nervous system so specialized and different from any other bodily system.

The brain has the greatest cluster of neurons in the entire body. A tiny slice of brain tissue the size of a grain of sand contains about 100,000 neurons. They are packed so tightly that a pebble-sized chunk of tissue from the human brain contains about two miles of neuron material. Your entire brain contains some 100 billion neurons, each one a fraction of a millimeter in size. To give you an idea of how many neurons this is, if you were to count to 100 billion, second by second, you would be counting for nearly 3,171 years. If you could stack 100 billion pieces of paper, the stack would be 5,000 miles high – the distance from Los Angles to London.

Other neurons are much longer than the nerve cells in the brain. Some neurons extend from the brain down the spinal cord and run up to three feet in length. Even though neurons vary in length, they essentially function in the same manner.

*To illustrate a few of the roles that neurons play in your life, imagine that it is morning, and you are planning the day ahead. As **your brain pieces together ideas** of what you will need to do during portions of your day, neurons transmit electrochemical information to and from various parts of your brain. **Sensory neurons send information to your brain not only about your external surroundings – via sight, hearing, smell, taste, touch, and pressure – but also about your internal environment, including sensations of hunger, thirst, pain, temperature, and so on.** Once you decide to get up and take action, motor neurons send electrochemical impulses from the brain through the spinal cord to the body, matching your movements with the mental plan you constructed.*

*The general method of communication between neurons is the same in all human beings. **However, nerve cells are organized in networks or patterns*** *that shape individual behavior and give us those unique difference we all possess.*

Needed to quote this part, since it was so well said that I couldn't in any way rephrase this explanation.

I'm giving myself a crash course here because it took me since 2005 to gather all this information and believe me I am still learning, since I need to remind myself often of what magnificent beings we are.

So the neurons are the ones that we train – with our thoughts – to fire into specific order. Something to think about, right?

The neurons connects themselves to each other – cluster – to reflect each situation that happens to us. The memory of those connections are gathered in our mind – consciously or subconsciously. Learning how to walk was conscious until it was learned and then place at the subconscious level. We don't need to remember how to walk, it is done automatically. As humans, we do not use the conscious level of our mind as often as we should. We don't stop and smell the roses any more. We are going at the speed of light at all times.

In our subconscious mind we also have repressed memories. Things that we have seen or learned and that we do not want to think about any more – if only that would be true. Regression is one of the human's most problematic issue. Unfortunately, even if we think that we are not subject to a past events in our daily routine, we are wrong. It is there and it is still affecting us. We need to be conscious again of these events and deal with them. This is where you might need the help of a professional – psychologist. Some repressed thoughts – emotions – are more harmful than a very sharp knife.

Here is a little story that happen to my daughter and me a few years back…

"CAN YOU THINK THAT YOU ARE A BIG PINK ELEPHANT?"

A very long time ago, my daughter and I were on a quest. Well, mostly I at that time since my daughter had fallen into a very bad mind trap – a polite way of saying a teenager's behavior. We were going from counsellor to counsellor not really getting anywhere, really. Most counsellors go with what they have learned and most of them go with the masses and surveys, not really going with the individual's need. Then there was this guy, Roland. Not a psychologist, not necessarily a graduate of any kind, however two things, which he would teach us stuck with me.

The first lesson he taught us was that life should be divided into 4 equal boxes:

FAMILY	WORK/ SCHOOL	FRIENDS	ME

After replenishing your own energy, you then can share your energy equally to each box. At that time, my "ME" and my "FRIENDS" boxes were almost none apparent.

FAMILY	WORK/SCHOOL	FRIENDS	ME

This was an ongoing problem for me. I am still, to this day, working on this. However, what is important is that I am aware of it and working on it every day. As of today, my friend box is still smaller than what it has ever been. I have, however, worked on the "ME" part. So, it's an ongoing thing.

FAMILY	WORK/SCHOOL	FRIENDS	ME

The second lesson that he taught us was that you can be anything that you want to be, in your mind. This is where it starts. That is where this question came up:

"CAN YOU THINK THAT YOU ARE A BIG PINK ELEPHANT?"

You can imagine anything you want. That is what distinctively separate us from the animal world. Our brain, specifically the frontal lobe, has the capacity to create thoughts more real than anything else.

This was to help my daughter to invent a new life so that she could eventually reach it.

**"All that we are is a result of
what we have thought."
Buddha**

At that time, it helped me a lot because this is where I started to imagine. Even though I was not necessarily believing that it could change me, I had a secret place to escape whenever I needed it. I could, and I still can, imagine that I am laying down on a sandy beach, enjoying the sun and the salty air, under a coconut tree.

Since that time, I have read many books, went to a lot of seminars, and I am still learning and enjoying the ride.

I have only understood what harm that I have done to my body, for those past 59 years just by rereading and understanding Joe Dispenza's books. He mentions in one of his books that when we try to change, we react much like an addict, because we become addicted to our familiar chemically induced states of being. Biblically explained, the flesh has taken over. He also states:

"Although we think or believe we are living in the present, there is a good possibility that our body and our thoughts are living in the past".

However, to reverse this might take some time, I would like to say that it takes less time than what it has taken my body to come to a bad state, to come to a point where you are back in charge. A little bit like knitting, if some can understand the analogy. Knitting a sweater takes some time. Unravelling it back to a ball of yarn is almost instant.

So the secret is to be aware of the harm that we are doing to our body. Just being aware is half the job done. It is not going to take me 59 years to **"FEEL GOOD"** again. I am feeling good right now.

Let's get back to more of a grey elephant... the brain.

So the brain can be manipulated by thought alone, but it is also directed by what our body needs. It seems that it is able to withstand a lot of demands but how far does this rollercoaster go? Can our emotions – or thoughts – become the catalyst of our destiny? The modifier of our structural being? And how would it happen? Because, yes, they do... and we need to become aware of this.

Like I said before, our body is a protein making machine. There is also another form of structure made up of chains of amino acids called peptides. They are very similar to proteins. However, they are specific hormones created by the pituitary – in your brain – and gets order from the hypothalamus – also in your brain. They circulate in your body, through the bloodstream, and activate different glands, tissues, and organs. They are mainly activated by emotions.

Emotion: (1) a natural instinctive state of mind

deriving from one's circumstances, mood, or relationships with others. (2) Instinctive or intuitive feeling as distinguished from reasoning or knowledge.

The basic emotions are: happiness, sadness, fear, anger, surprise and disgust. They can easily be recognized and interpreted through specific facial expressions. They are normally associated with external stimuli but can easily be triggered by memories.

One of the effect of a negative emotion on the body is depression, which can cause a persistent feeling of sadness and loss of interest.

Since our main focus here is to "**FEEL GOOD**", our body constantly works very hard to try to keep us happy. However, our egotistical mind doesn't really know what true happiness is until we decide to feed it information about it, teach it.

When you do not know how your body works, it is very easy to fall into a depressive state and of course it is very hard to get out of it, too. Also, at this stage, medication is not the best solution. Awareness is. Since our neurons have created a cluster of this specific event, we need to re-wire our brain with a new happy event. Easy? No, but doable.

In our body, we have peptides that are trying to get us to do things that are in the best interest of us. All feelings/emotions are produced by four predominant peptides. Again, since our main purpose is to be happy, these peptides work together so that we are or become happy.

The first two peptides, endorphins and dopamine, can be self-induced.

The purpose of **endorphins** is to mask physical pain. Most runners have a boost of endorphins called the runner's high. Just when they think that they can't any more, a boost of endorphins gives them the strength to finish the race. It gives us endurance.

Dopamine is released when we have a feeling that we have found what we are looking for, or that you have accomplished something. This feeling you get when you cross out something off that long list of things to do. So the purpose of dopamine is to make sure that we get stuff done. This is why we need to write down our goals. We get dopamine out of it.

Some warning needs to come with dopamine because it is very highly addictive. Other substances that can release dopamine are alcohol, nicotine, gambling, and your cell phone...lol.

ADHD and ADD are frontal lobe disorders and have risen 66% in the past 10 years, mostly because it has been misdiagnosed as being a distractibility caused by an addiction that gives you a dopamine rush. When unbalanced, dopamine is very dangerous.

Key point: Committing in helping someone will help

you get rid of a dopamine addiction. Make it about them, not about you.

Fulfillment, love or trust are not managed by endorphins and dopamine. It's the job of serotonins and oxytocin. Because of these two, leaders fulfill their great responsibilities.

Serotonins are responsible for the feelings of pride and status. This is why we have events like graduations and other similar ceremonies. It makes your confidence rise. By getting recognized, you get a surge of serotonin. What is good about this event is that people that know you, that are proud of you, also get it.

It can also be triggered by acquiring "stuff" and raising your status by yourself, but it is not a true accomplishment since we need the relationship with others to achieve true serotonin rush.

The **oxytocin** is acquired through love, trust and friendship. It is very much acquired with physical contact. Example of this would be a mother giving birth or breastfeeding. Shaking hands with someone trustworthy. It is the human bond peptide/hormone. You get a rush of this when you do acts of generosity. This is why people would volunteer. Any act of kindness gives you oxytocin.

Good side effects of oxytocin would be that it prevents addictions, and boosts immune system. Happy people live longer. It increases creativity and solves problems. It is not addictive.

There is another peptide that is produced that is not necessarily good for our body, especially when it is produced in higher doses and on a constant basis. **Cortisol,** also named stress hormone, is supposed to be used in fright and flight situation. However, we humans are constantly into stress situation and this peptide is slowly killing us. Cortisol shuts down all possibilities of producing oxytocin and of course is shuts down our immune system.

So again, let's go into the nitty gritty of things... this is Joe Dispenza's narration from the movie "What the bleep do we know?"

> *The brain is made of tiny nerve cells called neurons. These neurons have tiny branches and connect to other neurons to form what is called a neuron net. Each place where they connect is incubated has a thought or a memory. The brain builds up all its concepts by the law of associated memory. For example: ideas, thoughts and feelings are all constructed and interconnected in this neuro-net and all have a possible relationship with one and other. The concept of feeling of love for instant, is stored in this vast neuro-net. But we build this concept of love from many other different ideas. Some have love connected to disappointment. When they think about love, they experience the memory*

of pain, sorrow, anger and even rage. Rage may be linked to hurt which may be linked to a specific person which then can be reconnected to love.

Who's in the driver's seat when we control our emotions? We know physiologically that nerve cells that fire together are wired together. If you practice something over and over again, these nerve cells have a long-term relationship. If you get angry on a daily basis, be frustrated on a daily basis, if you suffer on a daily basis, if you give reason for the victimization in your life, you are rewiring and reintegrating your neuro-net on a daily basis and now that neuro-net has a long-term relationship with all those other nerve cells called an identity. We also know that nerve cells that don't fire together, no longer wire together. They lose their long-term relationship. Because every time we interrupt a thought process that produces the chemical response in the body, those nerve cells that are connected to each other start breaking their long-term relationship. When we start interrupting and observing, not by stimuli and response and that automatic reaction, but by observing the effect that takes place, then we are no longer the body-mind-conscious emotional person that responds to its environment as if it was automatic.

There's a part of the brain that is called the hypothalamus. It is like a mini factory and it is a place that assembles certain chemicals that matches certain emotions that we experience. Those particular chemicals are called peptides, they are small chains of amino-acids sequences. The body is basically a carbon unit that makes about 20 different amino-acids, all together to formulate its physical structure. The body is a protein producing machine. In the hypothalamus, we take small chains of proteins called peptides and we assemble them into certain neuro-peptides or neuro-hormones that matches the emotional state that we experience on a daily basis. So there's chemicals for anger, and chemicals for sadness, and there's chemicals for lust. There's a chemical for every emotional state that we experience. And the moment that we experience that emotional state in our body or in our brain, that hypothalamus will immediately assemble the peptide and then releases it through the pituitary, into the blood stream. The moment they make it to the blood stream, it finds its way to different centers or different parts of the body.

Now, every single cell has these receptors on the outside. One cell can have thousands of receptors on its surface, kind of opening up to the outside world. And when a peptide docks on its side, it literally, like a key into a lock, sits on the receptor's surface and attaches to it and kind of moves the receptor, like a door bell buzzing and send a signal into the cell. A cell that has a peptide siting in it, changes the cell in many ways. It sets a whole cascade of bio-chemical events, some of which winds up with changes in the actual nucleus of the cell. Each cell is definitively alive and each cell has a consciousness particularly if we define consciousness has a point of view of an observer. There is always the perspective of the cell. In fact, the cell is the smallest unit of consciousness in the body.

A definition of an addiction is really simple: something that you can't stop. We give to ourselves situations that meet our chemical needs. An addict will always need a little bit more in order to get a rush, or a high of what they are looking for chemically. So the definition really means that if you can't control your emotional state, you must be addicted to it.

So the mind is when the brain is in action. If the brain is the instrument for intelligence, or processing thought, and mind is what the brain does, if you can improve how the brain works, who's doing the improving?

The answer is consciousness, our self-aware free willed individual that is really not the body, nor the brain and definitively not the mind.

The brain processes 400 billion bytes of information every seconds but we are only aware of about 2,000 bytes that have to do with the body, our environment and of course time.

So, of course it is very understandable why our body get sick. What we should focus our energy on is to find ways to change this unwanted event called sickness.

I have always been a person that wants to find a solution. What do we need to do to stay healthy or what should we do to get out of sickness?

Let's look at four major things that was found in people that had been healed. I am talking about major illnesses here, like cancer, heart disease, etc. with only the intent as a cure.

First, these people accepted the fact that there is an intelligence that lives within themselves, that somehow giving them life. They accepted, with the participation of Source, that they can manipulate or change the process of an illness or getting better. It's the same intelligence that makes your heart beat, digest your food, breaks down your food into nutrients for your cell to be able to take them in. Same intelligence that makes 10 million cells every second, and for a unique cell to go through 100,000 chemical reactions every second. Same intelligence that concocted DNA strands that are six feet long and fit in the tiniest of cells. If you would take the DNA strands of all our cells, you would have a ribbon that would go to the sun and back 150 times.

So, this intelligence that has assembled who I am, has a greater mind than I do cause I can't concentrate long enough on just my heart to beat, before I start thinking about what happen to work yesterday... lol. And, it sure loves me enough to put up with me and all the things that I have done throughout my life... grateful. So, that specific intelligence does not need me to manage anything, and I know that it exists.

Second, I need to believe that my attitude created whatever condition I am in right now. Every thought creates a chemical. So here's the bad thing. The moment you start to feel insecure, nervous, afraid, or sad, the next think you do is that you start to think the way you are feeling, which makes more chemical to feel the way you are thinking, and think the way you are feeling. Hope you get the picture.

It's a vicious circle. But what happens on the long run is that the **mind is now immersed in the body** because of all the chemicals produces by the brain. Remember. The mind is what the brain does and the chemicals are made by the brain, thus chemicals are a product of the brain activated by the mind which is very busy right now, and it has immersed the whole body of chemicals. We call this a state of being. The body should be the servant to the mind. However, when this happens, the mind is the servant to the body. And since the body is requesting more chemicals to stay in a sad state, let's say, the mind delivers. This is the creation of an addiction.

The next step, these people needed to acknowledge,

was that they needed to reinvent themselves, to change. "I have to become somebody else", "I cannot be this miserable person for the rest of my life". "I need to become somebody else".

Then they started to ask questions like: **"What would it be like to be a happy person?"; "who do I know in my life that is happy?"; "What would I have to change about myself to live in joy?"; "Who in history that I admire that was great?"; and "At what point did I lose it and believed that this is who I am?"**

The forth step was that, while they were rehearsing what they wanted to be, there were long moments that they lost tract of time. They lost themselves into a realm of pure consciousness where time doesn't matter.

So, to change what needed to happen, they needed their brain to make new connections. And, the two ways to make new connections in your brain is either by gaining new knowledge – those ah-ha moments that make your brain go "Well I didn't know about this. Let's investigate". The other way is to go through new experiences. While we go through these new experiences, our five senses collect data, and our neurons fire and re-wire to create new neuro-nets, then different peptides are born from new feelings and emotions.

Can this be done in a day's work? Nope. It takes sometimes longer to get out of a bad connections in our brain than to get into new one. However, the importance here is that you know better now and you can redirect your thoughts whenever you see yourself go into the wrong direction. **Now you know better**.

These intermittent breaks from the crappy you to a new you are more beneficial to your whole body than any medication you can find. If you can think, you can think positive. Don't let your body tell you different. Be the master of your body.

This is why I decided to write this book. Because when you are in a state of negativity, and you are sick, **sometimes you are such in pain that you cannot think straight**. Now I'll be able to take this book and look at this special chapter and of course the next one. Both of them for me will do the trick to regain enough awareness to take me back to where I want to be... to "**FEEL GOOD**".

You might be in a situation right now that you do not understand what is going on. I tell you. The best knowledge that you can acquire is anything about your body and your soul. It will enlighten you. **You will regain your sparkle**.

Now, maybe some of you have some kind of disease that doctors don't give you hope. I am here to tell you that they are no gods. The power that you have within yourself is directly linked with Source – God. To perceive you only need to believe. You are more powerful than any of those negative thoughts that have been implanted in your brain. They are only neuro-nets that need to be dismantled and replaced with new neuro-nets that will start the new production of what you need to "**FEEL GOOD**".

We are now going to enter the realm of the unseen or should I say almost never looked upon. The most powerful place that most humans do not understand and are scared of entering. Some, because of the beliefs they have now, will have great difficulty understanding. However, it is the key for humanity to evolve. It is where we do not need any material possessions or to be in charge. It is limitless, abundance in its pure form. The secret to all mankind which is at the tip of our finger, a grasp away from being completely free. When you have finally attained this place, you will want to go revisit on a regular basis. This place is called the "**present time**". Most of us live either in the past or in the future. It is time to reconnect with now.

What would it be like to be a happy person?

_____

_____

_____

_____

_____

_____

_____

_____

Who do I know in my life that is happy?

_____
_____
_____
_____
_____
_____

What would I have to change about myself to live in joy?

_____
_____
_____
_____
_____

Who in history that I admire that was great?

_____
_____
_____
_____
_____
_____
_____
_____
_____

At what point did I lose it and believed that this is who I am?

_____

_____

_____

_____

_____

_____

_____

Chapter 8

WHAT IS THE SOUL?

We live in a world with a multitude of characters and it is alright. What we need to understand, for our own sanity is that we are not here to change all of that. We are only here to change us, if need be. By changing us we start what we call a snowball effect. As the snowball goes down the hill, it will gather more snow. Some snowflakes will follow, others will be left behind and melt.

Most of us live either in the past or the future. Few live in the present moment.

Now, those that are in business will tell you: "This is not right. We cannot live in the present because we need to work towards our goals, towards our future". Nothing wrong in working towards a goal. But if you do it worrying about not them being achieved, that's not good either.

But the worst scenario are the ones that constantly live in the past. Moldering over something that was done to them 40 years ago. Telling people about their dilemma over and over again. Reliving every detail without leaving anything out.

You feel empathy for those people the first time they tell their story. But after hearing it over and over again, it just pulls you right into their nightmare. You do not want to be with those people any more. The best that you can do for those people is for you to be in your present time and your "**FEEL GOOD**" place. By showing them what life brings you, they might find a glimpse of what their life should look like.

What is happening in those people's brain is that the wiring and the firing of their nerve cells are into a pattern that needs to be changed – rewired. Very hard to understand when your own body is begging for more peptides of the sadness composition over and over again. Their body has taken charge. They are not in charge any more. Their body are addicted to the "sadness" peptides.

Why do I know all of this? Because I was one of those people. I was constantly angry at myself. It took me a long time to finally put the finger on the problem, but I was constantly reliving the past where I was told by my mother that I couldn't do anything right, I was worthless and I would never be worth anything. Am I completely cured? No. That's why I am writing this book. To remind me of who I really am. I am not someone's daughter. I do not belong to anyone. I am a unique individual, placed on this planet earth to learn things and to "**FEEL GOOD**".

Anyone that tells me that I am not going the right way, are only telling me that I am not going their way. Everyone on this planet as the right to do what they believe is right. My right may be wrong to you and, it's okay. Your right might be my wrong to me and it also is okay. This is where the concept "live and let live" comes into place.

As independent individuals, what we need to follow are simple steps so that what we do doesn't interfere into other individuals patterns. There are two sides of the medal, true. There is the dark and a bright side, yes. What is important is that you keep doing what makes you "**FEEL GOOD**". **Source will take care of the rest. It will bring about what you need as you go along.**

But before we get to the "**FEEL GOOD**", there are some steps that you need to follow. You might be in a state of despair and for now your main focus would be to get out of it. There are steps to get out of despair. You cannot jump from despair right to joy in one day. You need to heal the scares and re-wire your brain. You need to think about a new future, which has joy in it, and slowly get yourselves, step by step, to where you are going and to start feeling better. When you are starting to feel better, this mean that you are slowly re-wiring your brain to a better outcome.

It is possible that you might plunge back to your desperate state, but now you know that it is possible to go back to that higher step that made you feel better two days ago. So, you start climbing again, climbing out of bed with a bit of hope.

Sometimes, you look for others to help you. However, the one that really can help you is your true self. The one that is connected to Source – the Creator. You are part of that entity. You are co-creators. You can create new possibilities that will take you out of the slump that you are in. You just need to believe in your true self. If you can't believe in what you see in the mirror, go beyond that and believe in the one that is in the "meat suit" you see in that mirror. Always remember that what you see in the mirror is not (insert your name). It is a vessel to carry (insert your name). And since you need that vessel, the first step that you can do to help it, is to re-wire your brain with positive thoughts or better thoughts that you have in your mind right now.

There are only two kinds of thoughts: good or bad – positive or negative. We do name them.

Joy

Love

Appreciation

Passion

Happiness

Belief

Optimism

Hope

Contentment

Boredom

Pessimism

Frustration

Worry

Blame

Anger

Revenge

Hatred

Jealousy

Guilt

Fear

Despair

Positive feelings are joy, love, appreciation, passion, happiness, belief, optimism, hope and contentment. Negative feelings are boredom, pessimism, frustration, worry, blame, anger, revenge, hatred, jealousy, guilt, fear and despair.

When you are feeling in the negative way, you can only attract more negative situation. But, if you can, try to picture a glimpse of a positive possibility to come. Think of a time when you were happy. Focus on something joyful. I know it is very hard to do when you are at your lowest. However, it is how you start to go up to maybe feeling contentment or even hope, that you will be aware of a change in your body. Then you can continue having better thoughts, and feel better and better.

I find that when I am grateful for something, it really helps. Someday, I am grateful for the smallest things. A good cup of coffee in the morning, has always made me happy. Maybe for you, because of your health, this thought of a cup of coffee only reminds you of what your doctor has told you: "You shouldn't drink coffee in your condition". So, find another happy thought. I always joke about this but, if I had a doctor that would tell me not to drink coffee any more, I would find another doctor... lol.

You need to "**FEEL GOOD**" all the time. You might go through some episodes of your life that might not be in alignment with the "**FEEL GOOD**". I'm talking about death in the family, the loss of a good friend, or being betrayed by someone you trusted. But I am here to tell you that you need to get back to your happy place as soon as possible.

The worst moment in my life was the death of my father. It took me a long time to finally understand that he was here for the time that he was permitted to be here, with what he knew about being here. He was not aware of all I learned about how the brain works and how his body worked. He was also in a relationship with someone that was constantly negative. Although he seemed a happy person, there was the part of always battling someone else's battle. You cannot battle someone else's battles. They are not for you to deal with. We always want to help others. But, we need to help ourselves first before we can help others. You don't need others to feel good for you to "**FEEL GOOD**".

It's all in your mind – the good and the bad. Your mind can either keep you afloat or sink your ship. It is for you to choose. If you say that you are sad, you are right. If you say that you are happy, you are also right. It is up to you to shift your thoughts to the positive feelings list: joy, love, appreciation, passion, happiness, belief, optimism, hope and contentment.

Sometimes, the only person that can take you out of these big problems you have, is yourself. You might need the help of a professional for you to open your eyes on the situation. **The first step is awareness of the situation**. However, you are the only master of your destiny. Don't let the egotistical part of your mind believe that it is in charge, because it is not, unless you let it. Your true self is the observer of all what is going on and is able to shift that situation to what you really want: "**FEELING GOOD**". And you need to "**FEEL GOOD**" without material possessions, and without other people around you. You have to be the only person that can make you happy. Start by focusing on what you want and ignoring what you do not want.

What makes me happy is learning and sharing what I have learned. I love reading books, and not any kind of books. I am not into romance or science fiction or biographies. I love books that are very thick and are full of information regarding health, mind, quantum physics and also spirituality. For you it might be different. I need to learn more about this magnificent body of mine, how it works. **How can I help myself to better myself? What do you like?**

If you like a specific documentary and it helps you to be in your happy place, watch it over and over again. I sure do. I do not have a television right now, nor do I have internet. I stopped watching television, especially news, on September 11, 2001. I prefer reading or watching something that I have already read or watched than watching what is happening on the news right now. Depressing.

Now, others are going to say that you need to be kept informed. It's okay for them if that is what they want.

But they should not impose their beliefs on you. I don't want to hear over and over again that there has been a disaster somewhere on the planet. To hear it once is enough for me. Doesn't mean that I do not feel bad for those people and that I do not care. I just need to hear it once and I certainly do not need to hear it in a different version. It's the same tragedy. I keep away from bad vibes. However, I do put a good vibe – prayer – for them. That is the best I can do for them in the situation. Plastering Facebook with the same bad news is not going to make it better.

I enjoy discussing what I have learned with someone else that are in the same vibes as myself. If I start talking about spirituality with someone and they feel uncomfortable, that person is not someone that I should share my beliefs and my ways of being happy. That person has other things that might make him happy and I should accept that. But I shouldn't try to change that person's belief and likes to mine. I should instead find people that are on the same wave lengths than I. Kind of being on the same radio station. It might mean that I need to be alone for a while. It is better to be alone than to be with people that make you feel bad.

There are almost seven billion people on this planet. There are enough for me to find a few that are on the same wave length than I. Accept others as they are. Move on, if it is not in direct alignment with your "**FEELING GOOD**". Jesus said in Matthew 10:14

– "If anyone will not welcome you or listen to your words, leave that home or town and shake the dust off your feet". These wise words were written over 2000 years ago.

I have mentioned a lot of books, movies, and people in this book. I have referenced all of them at the end of this book for you to reach out to either buy them or view them on the internet. It's up to you. You can if you want to. I am not saying that you should absolutely watch them. It might not reach you the same way that it has reached me. However, there might be something in those books or movies that will trigger what you need to go farther and investigate and learn.

I had mentioned earlier in the book that what I was going to talk to you about in the end might not necessarily go with your own beliefs. I really need to talk about this because I believe that it is what made me want to go farther in life.

As I mentioned in the first chapter about Esther Hicks, in the movie "The Secret", she or should I say He opened my mind to another realm of possibilities. We are not alone. We are a collectiveness. Our soul – if it is how you want to name it – our true self is part of a collectiveness. Abraham, has Esther Hicks explains, is a group of entities. We are part of that group.

Part of what feeds our motivation are groups of thoughts that have already been recorded –

impregnated – in our mind, through groups of nerve cells – neuro-net. It might have been something that we have already heard before, or is it?

When I went to visit the medium in 2009, she showed me how to talk to that collectiveness. Yes, everyone can do it, not only Esther or myself. Not everyone will be able to achieve connection, but everyone could if they really want to. We are connected to that collectiveness even if we do not like it. Call it what you want. Like I said before, I call it Source, because it is the source to everything. You ask and you shall receive. Again, I quote the Bible. Matthew 7:7 – "Ask and it will be given to you; seek and you will find; knock and the door will be opened to you". Jesus understood.

It's like a radio. You need to be tuned into the frequency. However, to be in the right frequency, you need first to be in a positive state. Does not work if you are desperate, or fearful or frustrated.

The first part of this verse says "Ask and it will be given to you". Some people ask but they do not believe that it will be given to them. I was one of those people. Try it with something small first. Think about a friend that you haven't talk to in a long time; get to be invite for a cup of coffee; think about this new job that you want. It does work. You have to believe that you are going to receive it. Every time you ask, Source answers back. Maybe not right away but it will come. You just need to believe.

Meditation is something that also helps you to get connected to Source. I find that early in the morning or just before going to bed is a right time for me. However, I can get a connection anytime I want, if I want to.

Some people believe that meditation is a woohoo practice. It is just getting disconnected from all but Source. To get into a meditative state, just find a comfortable place. I like my office chair. It tilts just enough so that I am not laying down or sitting up. I close my eyes and concentrate on something simple: my breathing, the oscillating of a fan, the beating of my heart. In no time, I am in a meditative state. Pure relaxation. It might be hard for you at the beginning, but from one meditation to the other, you will find that you can be thinking of absolutely nothing for longer period of time. When you void your mind, this is when intuition comes in: what you really are looking for.

I have to come back to the subject of this specific chapter. The soul... What is the soul? How do you perceive it? Do you believe that it is only dedicated to yourself? Or like other religion believe: can be transposed to another body, animal or thing after the death of the body – the vehicle? Do you think that this soul is independent from other soul? Do you believe that it needs to perform by itself? Or can it be attached to something else? How do you see yourself?

I have been seeing myself as the daughter of someone and then the wife of someone else. I have never seen me for what I am. Yes, I do belong to something but not another human being. I am part of a collectivity. We all are. That bond is not visible though. It is what I have been calling Source. It is a collectiveness of all soul and that makes up what is called Source. It is not only made up of all the soul but everything that has energy, thus every form in the Universe.

At some point in my journals, there is a phrase that I had written when chatting with someone: "**It is time for Carole to take care of Carole**". It seems that there are two of us, but humanity only sees the "meat suit". Humanity acknowledge the form as being Carole. But there is someone or something else inside of us that acknowledges the form, Carole. Our true identity, is the one that is observing Carole writing this simple phrase: The one that sees the form in the mirror. The true Carole. Who really loves that true Carole? The one inside? Now let's go deeper... I can love that Carole... now who is "I"? We are not only two but kind of three battling for identity. There is the body, which is recognized by the masses; there is the egotistical part of the mind that is created throughout our life; and there is the true person, the energy that flows through us, the part that is the most important part, the part that is not acknowledged by many.

I read a phrase in Eckhart Tolle[16] book, "The Power of Now"[17] which intrigued me: "**If you could bring intense presence into your aloneness that would work for you**

too". Aloneness is something that we create. I don't call it like that anymore. I call it my solitude. Solitude is generated by yourself. Aloneness is created by your mind – you believe that you have to be in the presence of others to be happy. I like my solitude – being without other human beings – to "bring intense presence" – the Collectiveness. I am never alone any more. I feel that intense presence of the Collectiveness. It guides me. It keep me company any time I summon it. Scary? It was for me when it was introduced to me.

In this Collectiveness are all souls: past, present and future. The ones that appeal to you come forth and talk to you – this would be a way of putting it, I guess. They can come at any moment and put a thought in your thought pattern.

You are at the coffee shop and you are reading a book, and all of a sudden, something takes you out of what you are doing with a thought of a person that you have not seen for a while. A few days later, you cross that person on the street.

You leave home every morning through the same route, but this morning you find yourself going another way. You start saying to yourself: "What is the matter with me? Why the heck did I go this way, it's longer?" Then when you finally cross the place that you usually go through, there is an accident and there is a long line up of cars, which you would have been in if you would have taken the same route.

You are talking with someone on the phone, and that person asks you to come to an interview right away. You refuse because you had planned something else. You only go the next day, and then you do not get that position because someone else went yesterday and got it. You find yourself getting another job that you like better and pays better.

This is all part of the Collectiveness trying to guide you in the direction that they have chosen for you. The right path.

The movie "The Secret" was not only a gift from my friend in Sherbrooke. It was a gift from the Collectiveness. It open my eyes to a totally new world that I hadn't had a chance to explore because of pure fear. When you say "no" sarcastically to something, it is not intelligence that is guiding you, but fear. It brought me to Joe Dispenza to explore the brain more. It also brought me to Esther Hicks and the Teaching of Abraham. It introduced me to Dr. Michael Beckwith, to the Revelation 2018 in California and of course to the publisher of this book.

It also knew how to proceed regarding mediums and channeling because I was very skeptic regarding that subject. It introduced me to a friend in Moncton that was open to such knowledge who had a friend in New Maryland that did channeling.

I have to talk about something that happened to me

in the past. I used to be able to predict things that would happen. But my mother was scared of this and told me to stop. So, I never really explored it more. My father would read books of Edgar Cayce[14]. He was a very open-minded person. Just to say, that it was introduced to me a very long time ago, but at that time I didn't grasp it, I wasn't ready for it, it was not the right time. The Collectiveness didn't give up on me and came back, strongly. This time, I was more prepared, I think.

Nine years ago, I discovered this energy that is eternal – the Collectiveness. It had been tugging at my heart but never really acknowledged it. It was randomly introduced to me through a series of introductions. Everything happens to us for a reason.

Mid-August 2009, I was at my friend's home in Moncton. My spouse was in Montreal for a week or so, and I decided not to go. I wanted something different for a vacation, not doing the same old thing year after year. So I came down to see my friend for a few days.

On Friday morning, she got a call that she needed to go to work that afternoon. So it meant for me to go back home. For some reason, I thought of her medium friend in Fredericton. She said that it would be kind of impossible for me to get a meeting with her in such a short notice. Well, I still called. You never know, and I could at least schedule a date.

She answered on the first ring and said that I could see her that afternoon. She also said something that now I understand: "**We are waiting for you**". At that time, "we" for me meant a lot of people, but wasn't she supposed to be alone when she was doing the channellings?

So, I started to drive towards Fredericton. Got there about 45 minutes before my time. I waited patiently in the car. I didn't want to be too fashionly early. I wasn't waiting ten minutes that a beautiful tall slim blond woman came out on the front steps and waived at me saying: "Come in, we are waiting for you".

She mentioned something about over 150 people that wanted to speak to me and in my mind I acknowledged a sarcastic remark about her maybe being a quack. We went to a study downstairs. She sat on a sofa and I sat on another one squared to hers. She prepared her laptop because she did record the session so I would have a CD of the recorded session. She explained a bit of what she was doing and started.

It didn't take her long before she was in a somewhat trance and I was introduced to Archangel Michael. During this session there was also Archangel Raphael – my favorite of archangels – Mary Magdalen, Jesus of Nazareth and St-Francis of Assisi.

I was very emotional. There were things that were said to me that I couldn't imagine her knowing. She mentioned that the ringing in my ear was caused by the multitude of people that want to talk to me from the Collectiveness. How could she know about that ringing? Only my doctor knew about it. She certainly didn't have a relationship with my doctor. A lot of questions were going through my mind.

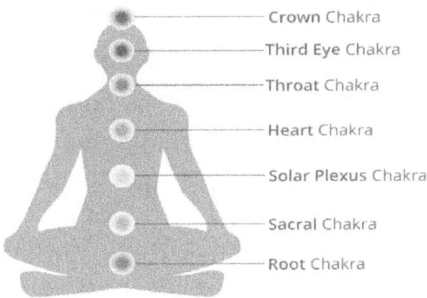

Crown Chakra
Third Eye Chakra
Throat Chakra
Heart Chakra
Solar Plexus Chakra
Sacral Chakra
Root Chakra

At one point in the session, I was very emotional. We were talking about my dad. She asked me to go to a big plate near a fire place and choose a stone. When I got to that big plate made of some kind of marble, there were hundreds of crystals. I love amethyst. So I was going through them trying to find an amethyst but this rounded **pink crystal** kept coming back, so I took that one.

I had it in the palm of my hand, my hand was closed over it and she said:

"You have chosen the pink quartz because... ". Well, the better was getting better... lol. I was working a lot with women at that time. Doing seminars for women's health, selling bras, and mostly meeting women for consultations. Pink is the color of the 4th **chakra**. Chakras are centers in our body believed to be psychic energy centers in the esoteric traditions of Indian religions. The forth chakra is normally associated to the color green but the pink quartz is also associated to it.

It is the center of love, compassion, harmony and peace. The Asians say that it is the house of the soul. This chakra is in direct association with your lungs, heart, arms, hands and thymus gland.

So, to continue what she was saying: "You have chosen the pink quartz because we like what you are doing with women" – the bra fittings, seminars and health consultation.

She then told me that I needed to converse with the ones that wanted to talk to me. "How???" She explained to me that I needed a gate keeper, since I had so many people that wanted to speak to me at the same time, it was difficult to decipher what was said to me, thus the ringing in my ear. So, since I like St-Raphael, I decided that he would be my gate keeper. I needed to find a comfortable position. It could be sitting up or lying down but it was important that my head was higher than my heart. She told me to place my left hand on my heart and my right hand on my belly. She told me how to relax: close my eyes, breathe slowly, concentrating on my breathing, my heart beat, the oscillating sound of a fan. Then feel my body disconnect – my feet, my legs, continuing upward until I didn't feel my body any more. Then I would ask my gate keeper to let just one entity at a time to talk to me. I decided that I would do this tonight when I got home. We continued to chat, all of the five entities, the medium and I, and then I parted.

Here is a passage of this reading I had with that medium.

You are a healer of hearts, you are known to us since the beginning of time, beginning of hope and humanity on this planet. There is this woman within you that looks like and ankh. **Do you know what an ankh is?** *You are known to us in the name of the ankh, in the name of oneness. This ankh is inside of you in your entire physicality. At this moment your body is unhappy. It feels the excitement of who you are, does not understand why you are not expressing it. It wishes you to go within and to pursue passion and go and* **follow courses to learn how to express the beauty of your soul.** *This be what it wishes of you and for you. You are not fully grounded like wise. And so we would ask you when you meditate to start with candles and burning of incent and start to pray and we would ask you before you start to pray, to breath and yet as we breath as we did this day, breathing normally hand over heart and then three deep breath in through* *heart and then through feet and feel deep root sending deep down planet earth. You are not fully grounded for you are a being of light and you are not comfortable with other people selfishness and you are taking this on as something that you have*

done to allow them to hurt you. You understand? That is inappropriate. What is appropriate is the grounding of your root and the placing of the **buoy of light** *and you will see what a beautiful creature Carole is and the physicality will shift. And they say (laughing) that you will become a* **lean mean feisty machine** *too. Your spirit is extremely strong and extremely wise and says it is about time, and it is looking at his watch, and says it is about time that she came to see us.*

So, the session ended and I started driving back home. I couldn't put the radio on. I just couldn't believe what just happened to me. The only thing that would come out of me about every 15 minutes of the three and a half hour drive was: "Wow".

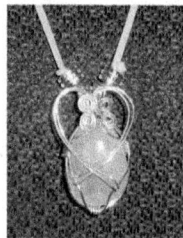

The other thing that I could think about was that **pink crystal** and the desire to do a wrapping with it when I got home. When I finally did, it only took me 20

minutes to do this creation. Then I decided to follow the medium's information – or should I say Archangel Michael's information – to reach out to those who needed to speak to me.

I was still alone that evening and to this day I am so grateful for that, because what happened that evening, changed my perception of everything.

So, I laid down in our queen size bed, put up a pile of pillows so that my head would be comfortably higher than my heart. I put my left hand on my heart and the other one on my belly. Relaxed. Started to disconnect my body, slowly and then when I finally felt like if I was floating, I asked Archangel Raphael to let one in...

Well... talk about a jolt of lighting. My body became stiff as a board and then it arched and I let go a scream. "That's it! I'm not doing that shit any more", I said to myself, and ran into the kitchen. I was scared. I didn't know what had happen to me. I need to speak to someone about this, but who? I thought in calling the medium but it was late. I sent her an email. She replied right away. She reassured me that I was doing the right thing and to continue doing it. She told me that I just had my first connection with the Collectiveness. I was very tired and couldn't do it again. I fell asleep and had a real good night sleep.

The next evening, since I was alone again, I took courage and tried again. And this is when I was introduced to

Phylea. Everything happened like the night before, but this time when I got that bolt of lightning through my entire body, I cried out Celia. In my mind I thought I had heard Celia, but she came back and said: "No, Phylea" and spelled it, P-H-Y-L-E-A, in a very aggressive tone as if she was mad at me not understanding the first time. Then for me that was enough for that evening. I had to let the medium know what was going on. So again, I fired up an email and she answered back and told me to continue investigating and to journal what was happening to me.

I started asking questions and writing down what she would tell me. I came to a point where I could relax my body anywhere and converse with her. I also would sit in front of my computer and type what she would tell me. Here are one of those readings I had with her. This specific reading was on Tuesday, August 25, 2009 8:00am.

Q: If each entity would make peace with himself, life would be a wonderful experience. When did this break? If at one time love and harmony prevailed on planet earth, what happened that it stopped?

> **A:** *The human body is equipped with a guiding system. It also has the ability to make choices for itself. We are like two entity in the same ship. One must first make peace with the other. If the other (speaking of the ego) questioned the other about the guidance it has been given, it can also make*

choices. The choice may not be in accordance with the guidance that was offered when the human being was born (or way before that time it was given). Many human preferred to go with other choices, thus not having peace within their own hearts. When someone is not at peace with himself, wars emerge. Small ones at first and then massive ones that destroys whole worlds. On planet earth, there has been many time that there were highly regarded population. But like at any time, the ego stepped in and worlds collapsed.

Q: Who are you?

A: I am now speaking to you has being Phylea. I lived in a world that was very prosperous and rich in human kindness. Everyone had everything they needed. There was no need to feel (like with the ego) smarter or richer than others. Everyone was equal in all aspects. Everyone had the ability to heal themselves because they knew that it was possible and there was no worries to the contrary. Life was the essence of all.

But there was not only our tribe. Another tribe was also like us before but didn't want to follow their guiding system. They wanted more and more and collect material that made them feel stronger and bigger. So our world ended at the hand of that tribe. What I tell you is because you asked but it has no importance to you or what you are experiencing today. The only important matter is to be in harmony with self. When in harmony with self, nothing matters, nothing hurts. There are many that are now understanding this self-harmony. You are meeting some every day. You can feel them, you have that ability. You are in a learning process now, kind of. You need to keep your strength to yourself, since you are weak, spiritually wise. You need to declutter you whole life. You may ask questions about your own evolution now. Soon, you are going to help other do the same decluttering of their own lives. But you need to help yourself first.

Q: What do you suggest?

A: We have been telling you what to do for a long time. We are not being mad at you or reprimanding you but we have been giving you images and taking you to places you should have understood. You live in a beautiful area. You know it because you admire it often. The river, the birds, beautiful scenes. You are also close to the sea. Many trees around your home. Feel free to sit close to the river and close your eyes and reflect and many ideas and pictures are going to appear. We had shown you an area not so long ago where you should go as often as you can. You are a beautiful soul and you love all beautiful things. (Re-reading this made me think that I am not living in a beautiful place any more, sadly. So, I decided to start looking around for another place similar to that place, and travelling. Meanwhile, I will decorate my tiny space, amongst chaos, with flowers, lights and maybe a little fountain to bring about my liking of being close to waters.)

Q: Who am I?

A: You are you. You are part of a collectiveness. You are part of me as I am part of you. We are all one. No one is by himself. But you are asking what you could have been like the name I told you, and my story. You have a very old soul. You have experience the collapse of two worlds already and that has giving you a bad feeling in your heart. Right now you are seeing and experimenting experience of yet another collapse of the world. This one will be very small compared to the two others, but still it will be a collapse and you can feel it. But this time as a human being you will be ready and as a soul you are going to be ready. Because you know that there is no end to collectiveness and this collectiveness will save this world from going through a massive end like the two others you have experienced.

Q: How can I get more energy, because lately I am so tired? I feel like sleeping all the time.

A: You have experience to much of the egotistic ways of the human being. You have experience that not so long ago and it has broken your heart. You have difficulty understanding why people would do *such harm to others. But you have to understand that these measures that others take to overpower themselves are indeed weakening themselves. When comes time of great movement in the world, they will be alone in their egotistical world. They will not be able to survive, spiritually. They will be running like chicken without heads. But you do not need to worry about them right now. We need for you to be stronger spiritually and be strong for others that will accept the change, **for there is change to come**. If you need to sleep, sleep. If you need to eat, eat. If you need to go for a walk, go for a walk. For a few months you will need to do what you feel like doing to strengthen your body and mostly your spirit. You will go see the person named Pam more often, at least once a month. She will give you tips how to understand what you are going through.*

Q: How can I avoid people that can hurt me like what happened in Campbellton? (I had a very bad situation that happened to me at work. A disgruntled employee.)

A: All human have a lot of problem with these kind of situations. We are not reprimanding you, just informing you. What happened yesterday should in no way affect today, spiritually wise. Words or actions of yesterday are but fog blown away by the winds of change. But, you (spoken as a collectiveness of the human beings) remind yourselves of the past, and others question you *about the past. It becomes a daily habit. You need to change the story to a story that makes you **feel good**. To avoid those people, imagine your buoy of light surrounding you at all time. This is what you should do at least for the next 4 months. People are going to ask you questions about what you are going through, because you have spoken to some and they will ask. There are some that you can trust. Some only wants to know for their own benefits. But you're not ready for them. You must work on yourself first.*

Q: Is there any way to know what kind of person they can be before you get hurt?

A: Your heart never lies. It has always told you. You will be able to master this gift as you go along. You have a good heart. You trust every one. You sometime trust too much. You do paint pretty pictures but there are some in that pictures that do not belong there and they do not match the color of your dreams. Continue with your buoy of light around you. You care too much about others now. Turn that care to yourself and your light will get stronger and stronger. You can feel us very easily. You can call upon us at any time for answers, comments. Ask us anything and we will guide you, if this is your will. Do what you have to do to survive (work). Do what you have to do to live (love). Do what you have to do to exist (feel good). We work well together, don't you agree? Your meditation and us talking to you to transcribe in typing. A wise thing to do would be to save on to something that you can read often. For reading what we write makes you stronger, makes you feel good.

(Went to the bathroom)

You just took a break and we were still there to answer your questions, you noticed? During the day when you have a question and you do not want to forget, write it down (manually). It will be easier for you to remember the question when you come back at us. You have been asking all the time and we have been answering all the time. You have just not understood it as of now. The answers were treated as far fetch (some) and you released the thoughts but they were the answer for that question, every single time, no mistake, this was the answer. You will understand more of what we are conversing together as we go along. Listen to Pam's reading again and again. Write what she is saying (or what we are saying to you through Pam). It will give you strength. The more you understand your gift, the more you will regain your strength and you will become stronger than before because you will have mastered your gift. Now you are a bit confused, scared of speaking to others and it is normal. Soon you will have no more fear, no more doubts. You can feel it through you surging some time. But you are stopping the process because of doubt. We are so excited for you. We are so happy to see that you are joining us, not that you had ever left us but that you can join us both spiritually and physically. You will find more and more time to work like you are doing now and it will go faster and faster as we progress. Some will help you as you go along, like Pam.

Q: Are there any others that I can trust to help me go through this?

A: You have two friends that have the power to do the same. One has experienced it strongly. One is very hyper (as you would say) the other one is very low key (as you would say). Both can bring you great help through what you are going through right now. They will not be able to subside to temptation and it is normal that they would like to know about themselves, but you will need to work on you first, and only you. Tell them to be patient, time will come for them and you will also help others greatly.

Q: Lately, and mostly in the last few days, I have been dreaming about beautiful places, exotic places. There is lots of light and warmth. Veils, beautiful dresses in light colors. Beautiful women, laughing and helping each other's and helping others in need. Soft skin, perfumes, smelling good. I see no men around at all. Beautiful jewelry. Just beautiful all over. What can I relate to that?

*A: I would suggest that you speak with Pam and mostly Princess Hatshupset. (Entity that speaks to Pam as Phylea speaks to me.) They will enlighten you with this. What we can tell you is that you were part of the sisterhood at one time. You were part of its decline. This is why your heart is broken. You are yourself a creator. You do like to make things. That gives you pleasure. Your work is satisfying, in one way only: pleasing the others. You enjoy beautiful things: clothes, jewelry, perfumes. These things lack in your world now. But they are not important they are material things, but you would enjoy them as gifts. You can also make what you desire, isn't this another great gift? You need to please Carole. She deserves it. When dreaming of these dreams you "**FEEL GOOD**", and the main thing is "**FEELING GOOD**". Either it is having those items or dreaming about them, for you, it is the same feeling. So think about those things. You were wearing beautiful jewelry when you were in the sisterhood. You see them. Draw them and make them. That will please you a lot. You see garments too. Draw them and make them. Wear them too. You are never alone. We are always with you. Never consider yourself as being alone. You can talk to us always. Your relationship will change very soon and many people will fill those spaces that you call empty. Joy will be and abundance, and this is what it should be. We have changed the subject a bit because this is something that is bothering you also. You believe that you are all by yourself but you are not. You are not alone.*

I have drifted away from Phylea. I am sorry to say that. But I know that she is always there – they are always there, and I am part of that Collectiveness. I am not alone any more. I feel them tugging at my heart, but I do not always answer back or follow their guidance and I am sorry about that too. But, by writing this book to me, I am already feeling the strength coming back to me, day by day. I know that this is part of their willingness to help me and I am forever grateful about them. I need them more now that I have ever needed them and they know it. They are not mad at me for not being conscious of them constantly. They hold no grudge like us humans. I do need to learn about what is my path on this planet at this time. It is a learning process. Each of us need to know that. We are living a life of learning. Our true self, which is connected to the Collectiveness, are here only to observe how we are going to go through this life with this body. But, if we are willing to listen to them, it could be a whole lot different than what it could be or what we anticipate it to be.

By reading this special passage I had with Phylea, it has given me the urge of creating again. I am going to start sewing again and make beautiful clothes. I love veils, and light materials. I love clothes that are not clinging to me and tight. I like seeing my clothes flowing in the wind. I have started to experience different essential oils again. I have them in my home but didn't quite used them at their fullest lately. Thank you Phylea, Collectiveness, Universe, and Source, to have made me go in that direction again. Thank you!

I hope that this didn't scare you off. Like I said at the beginning, this book is for me. This works for me. Phylea or the Collectiveness is always there for me, I know. I seem to get away from it, as if I forget about it. Then I read this passage again, and I get all energized again.

We, humans are all able to go through what I have gone through. We all have the ability to listen to our God, our Collectiveness, or our Source. What we lack is awareness and the willingness to just listen. Women are mostly able to do this more easily that the majority of men. It has to do with how our brain is wired.

Since I started to work on this book and written this special chapter, it has given me the strength and courage to write about my special project again. You see, when I was taking my Natural Health Practitioner course, I had mapped out, to my knowledge, what we need to keep this vessel of ours, our "meat suit", in good condition. I call it my "Flower of Hope". So, I decided to add it to my book. I hope that this "Flower of Hope" will help you as much as it has helped me to bring back my body to a better fighting chance with the life's circumstances...

NOTES

Chapter 9

WHAT IS MY FLOWER OF HOPE?

Disease is a healthy body with extra baggage. Take away the excess baggage and you have a healthy body again. People tend to do the contrary. Instead of finding what is in excess, they add more. So we take antalgics or analgesics, antacids, antibiotics, anticoagulants, aspirin, barbiturates, beta blockers, bronchodilators, corticosteroids, diuretics, histamine, hypnotics, laxatives, neuroleptics, and tranquilizers to name a few.

We never lost our health. It's still there under all that camouflaged, chemically induced, false healing potions that we take without questioning the giver. Our body fight all the time for us to keep us alive, even though we bombard it with manmade chemicals that only halter our perception of the disease, or even brings in more symptoms, which of course would need more chemicals for our body to try to dissipate. For some, it ends quickly. For others, it lasts many years. Many years of pain and confusion. Some will continue seeing the same doctor, plus a hand full of specialists to their dying breath.

We have lost the ability to read and understand our symptoms and to give what our body really needs.

We have put trust into people that also have lost these abilities.

As per the medical field, we are categorized into two groups: "the ones that needs their services, and the other group, the ones that will eventually need their service, because a healthy person is only a potentially ill person to the eyes of this big business".

I would like to quote Dr. Christiane Northrup[13] on this system that we have right now, because it is pretty accurate. She says:

> "This is really important. We don't have a Health Care System folks, we have a disease screening, disease care, crisis intervention, pharmaceutical maintenance system. It doesn't really have to do with health at all except to bring you back from the jaws of death. It's very good for acute care. It runs on fear and doesn't acknowledge the wisdom of an illness or the wisdom of a symptom you might have. The crisis intervention mode is this: Think of a health care system as a raging river with rapids and doctors and the health care system are in power boats running out into the rapids grabbing the drowning victims and resuscitating them in high rise buildings called hospitals where they are then triaged to pharmaceuticals maintenance for the rest of their lives. That's most of that. Then there's the better chemistry approach to health and this

is that you can't go through live without being on at least one or two prescription drugs.

I spent my whole life in the rapids, getting very good with the power boats. I could steer those babies and refuel them and I could work in the high rise thing and then I said: "You know what? Why don't I go upstream and see why people are jumping off the bridge, in the first place, or at least see who's pushing them off.

We need more doctors like Christiane Northrup. The system is full of doctors that are only there for the pay. They don't even want to touch you anymore. I remember when I was younger, when it was time for a checkup, there were no getting out of it, and you had to strip. Now, they are just listening to what you are saying and waiting to hear where it hurts and making sure that the prescription pad is used. Sure some have been caught in some sexual harassment cases and possibly that is why doctors won't touch patients anymore. I understand that there can be faulty beings on both sides. But when you are complaining about pain and they don't even touch or look, how can they prescribe something for what?

I am not saying that we don't need them at all. They are very good on our final time on earth and when you have to go through an operation, they are quite busy and present. Besides that, they are what Dr. Northrup described above.

Went a bit negative here, and I apologize. However, the "Health System" shouldn't be called that. It should be called "Crisis System". A health system should do what they advertise: "Health". And by that I mean health education, at all levels: Body, mind and soul.

What we need to repeat ourselves is that "our body has the capacity to heal itself given the necessary and natural elements such as food, air, water, exercise, plenty of rest, etc." It knows how to defend itself without the help of any vaccines. It knows how to, without us telling it. It is a marvellous machine.

A cold is merrily a way for your body to tell you that it's lacking antioxidants. A diarrhea is your body expulsing rapidly what is not needed in your body. If you have constipation, then that expulsion is difficult and the causing agent of a disease might not be expulsed. Afterwards, the disease will incubate and show up at a later date.

When I took the Natural Health Practitioner course I was fascinated. At that time, I unfortunately had gone true many different diseases and also was without a few parts that were removed instead of investigated. What were they telling me? What is it that I was doing wrong or had done wrong to be in that state? Unfortunately, this was not just a few weeks ago but a full 46 years of uncaring for my body and following whatever diet that was given to me as a child and what I had learned from generations of non-education in the health department.

Even though I was 46 years old and a few part missing, there were still lots of things that I could start now and then, to help my body to heal itself. With that course, I helped my body to regenerate itself! This is when my vision became:

"Help your body to regenerate itself".

I also worked on what would be my mission. Being without some body parts, I asked myself if it was possible to be healthy, and the answer is yes. Your body is a very intelligent machine. It will retrieve what it needs from other parts of the body when needed. Did you know that even though you have a total hysterectomy (removal of uterus and ovaries), your body can still retrieve the precious hormones from your adrenal glands? Of course, you need to know that and you need to have a healthy body so that will happen. If you suffer from what doctors call "adrenal fatigue", your adrenal glands are already maxed out. At this point, for you to be able to retrieve those precious life giving hormones, is almost impossible. So, my mission became:

"To put the individual's well-being in harmony with life's circumstances."

As individuals, we constantly change through the course of time and circumstances. We need to adapt to what is places in front of us. However, we are always challenged with what our body needs and this is why

I have sat down at the very beginning of my course to find a way to understand these needs and to be able to explain these needs easily to others.

So this is how I came with my *"Flower of Hope"*. I consider myself as a "Hope Dealer". It makes people chuckle a bit when I tell them that, and it also puts them at ease when we get to explain this marvellous six step process to a healthy body.

At first glance it seems that they are all individual subjects. However, they are all intricately intertwined and each one is needed for your body to function properly, thus being healthy.

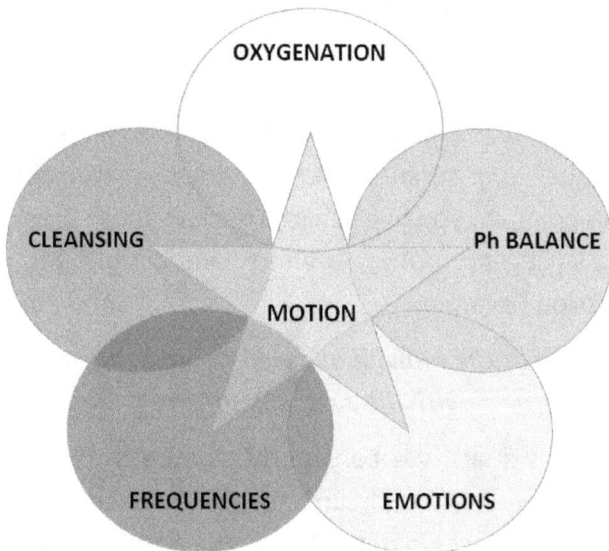

FACTS ABOUT WATER

Water is one of the main constituting elements of living matter and is the vehicle for all exchanges in the body. Over 60% of the body is made up of water, which means that a man who weighs 70 kg is made of 42 kg of water.

Water is eliminated in different ways. The daily assessment of water in the body includes losses through:

- The skin (vapour) and lungs (0.5 %),
- In excrements (4.5 %),
- And in urine (approximately 1 litre or 95 %).

The body requires a daily supply of **2.5 to 3 litres** of water to compensate for losses (**drinking water and water contained in food**). A good way to determine how much drinking water we should have per day, would be to divide our body weight (in pounds) and drink that amount in ounces. (Ex: you weight 150 lbs – you should drink 75 ounces of water.)

Digestive secretions (including water and what we have eaten) amount to nearly 10 litres per day and are reabsorbed by the small intestine and the colon.

A small amount of this water is formed within the cells and results from the oxidation that occurs there; however, most of the water in the body comes from beverages and food.

VERY IMPORTANT: Water can also be absorbed by the skin while taking a shower or bath. This questions the soaking therapy in bath water and mineral salts. While soaking, you are not only absorbing the salts and the water, but also what is in the water. Chlorinated water is not necessarily the best water to be absorbed by your skin. Whatever benefit that you get from the salt, will be counteracted by the harm that the chlorinated water is doing to your body. Soaking in chlorinated water is not a healthy solution. Having a massage to activate the lymphatic system and drinking water would be more beneficial than soaking in chlorinated water.

- Total water = 60 to 70% of body weight.

- Plasma water (water contained in the blood vessels) = 4.5%.

- Extracellular water = 16% of body weight.

- Total fasting can lead to a 9% weight loss in two days, 5% on the third day, and then 1.5% the following days. (However, this should not be done without the consultation of your practitioner).

- Two elements are necessary for the body to cleanse itself:

  - Plant fibre – To accelerate digestion and help form stools.

  - Water – To help produce urine.

- The amount of water contained in the food we eat varies. For instance, hazelnuts contain 5% water and cucumbers contain 75%.

Without water, our body would not be able to eliminate toxins from our body. It is a very important part of the cleansing process of our body.

The quality of the water you drink is also very important. The best water to drink would be the water coming from a well, as long as it is checked very often to verify potential threat or pathogens. The pH levels of the water is another important matter, which we will be discussing a little bit later. If it is possible, filtering the water is important. Bottled water are not necessarily the best because of the untrustworthiness of certain company. It is very important that you do your homework and find a trustworthy company. Filters come in a variety of prices. One that is not that expensive can be purchased from the Brita family, where you can install directly on the faucet. This is a $50 investment and eventually the filter needs to be replaced at the cost of $25.

I have invested in a brand where the water is filtered and the pH is balanced. It is up to you to do the math and see what better suits your needs and also doesn't go to deep in your finances.

A body that is well hydrated, will be cleansed and no disease lives in such a body.

FACTS ABOUT AIR

We don't really think about this one much during the hours of one day. Unless we have some kind of disease, we breathe in and out automatically without any effort. This wonderful Force that we are not so much aligned with does all the work for us.

But put disease in the body and things start to change. We never notice it but we alter the way we breathe when we are sick. If we would take only five minutes a day and really put our attention on the way we breathe in and breathe out, our body would be very grateful.

When we breathe in, there are millions of chemical reactions going into our body. Some toxins are dislodged and it is here, where I was saying, that all six elements of the Flower of Hope is important: water will cleanse de body of those toxins that are dislodged.

On your days off, give yourself the gift of fresh air. If you live in a city, go for a long drive in the country and just breathe. This is a free gift and your body will thank you for this.

When meditating, be aware of your breathing. Reteach your body to breathe. Be aware of your breathing many times a day. Notice how your body appreciate that you are aware of the breathing. Feel the air go in and out.

**There are no disease living
in a well oxygenated body.**

FACTS ABOUT pH

pH is a way of measuring the body's acidity or alkalinity. It is measured between 0 and 14. From 0 to 7 the body is acidic; 7 is neutral; and from 7 to 14 the body is alkaline. Not only is the body tested with this formula. The dirt is tested to grow different produces. Your pool is tested so that you do not have any algae. This is a part that the doctors don't really look into, that they do not understand much.

What most people are is acidic. We do not drink enough water. Whatever liquids we have inside becomes stagnant and like a lake that is stagnant or dormant and develops algae, our body develops all kind of disease.

Acidity in the body augments through years of malnutrition, not enough hydration and of course low oxygenation. To rid the body of acidity takes some time. At this point, I would suggest that you go see a good Natural Health Practitioner so that you can discuss your individual situation. Since everyone is unique, it is impossible for me to give you the right recipe to success.

However, you can determine your pH level with Litmus paper which you can purchase at any pharmacy. This will determine your levels. You can test yourself early in the morning by either spitting on the Litmus paper of you can use your second pee, also in the morning. The best reading for pH would be between 6.8 and 7.2.

I will eventually have on my site a list of good food to eat to reduce the acidity in your body. But for now, I am just explaining what the "Flower of Hope" is by showing you each element rapidly.

**Again, disease doesn't live in a
well pH balanced body.**

FACTS ABOUT FREQUENCIES

For some, this part is a bit hard to understand. However, we are very energetic beings. Logically, if we are all made of the same thing – atoms, and atoms are full of energy, everything and everyone has a frequency signature. Some have a larger signature than others.

Frequency describes the number of waves that pass a fixed place in a given amount of time. ... Usually frequency is measured in the hertz unit, named in honor of the 19th-century German physicist Heinrich Rudolf Hertz. The hertz measurement, abbreviated Hz, is the number of waves that pass by per second.

The more alive you are, the more frequencies you dissipate. Our heart emanates large structural frequency patterns that can be measured across a room. Some people are very sensitive to energies of those kinds. I am. I can feel something happening before they do. Intent has a frequency signature. A thought has a frequency signature.

Coming back to the body... If you are in good health, you dissipate a larger number of hertz. If you become sick, less. Same for food. Good wholesome foods have a better hertz measurement than canned food, which by the way has none at all.

Emotions have a big impact on your hertz levels. A joyful person will emanate a big white aura while a sad person only has a small black lining around them. I say this because I do see them. Even though you might not see them, you can feel them. Stick around a negative person too long and you will feel their condition. To some it can make them sick, some just want to leave the room. What if you can't? What if you need to stay because it is your employment, you keep telling yourself?

The device to measure such frequencies is very expensive. But if you feel down, it is guaranteed that your frequencies are down. To help you get those back to a better levels would take some thinking. Petting your cat or dog can increase the levels of your frequencies. A good belly laugh, a walk in the woods, meeting a good friend are all good ways of increasing your frequencies.

The human body's best frequencies are between 62 – 78 Hz. If you have a cold or flu, your frequencies would be 57 – 60 Hz; cancer – 42 Hz. Even when the living spirit leaves our body, it would still generate 25 Hz.

Elevating or diminishing your frequencies can be as sensitive as holding a cigarette (- 17 Hz) to smoking a cigarette (- 23 Hz). Having a happy thought generates +10 Hz and praying /meditating +15 Hz.

Side note: Being a Natural Health Practitioner with

a specialization in Aromatherapy I was amazed to find out that 100% pure therapeutic grade essential oils do also have frequencies. I have seen some very interesting healing just by inhaling them.

Disease cannot live in a body with frequencies between 62 – 78 Hz.

FACTS ABOUT EMOTIONS

This delicate petal of the "**Flower of Hope**" needs to be considered as being the key to many unanswered questions. Emotions are only starting to be understood. The correlation between disease and emotions are now being more and more seen. You can, without investigating, believing that they do. However, I have always been the person that need to really find the "why", and I had to really go down the rabbit hole with this subject.

Emotions can destroy the body as it can heal the body. I mean respectively negative and positive emotions. Having negative emotions can cut your air supply, bring down your frequencies and pH levels. When a person stays in a state of sadness, anger or despair too long, the body becomes the master and demands more and more of the respectful peptides to stay in that state.

To get out of that slump, you first need to be aware of what is happening and then greater willingness to help your body's addiction to get out of it. When knowing what you are doing to your body, is sometimes not enough because if you are in a very deep depression, sometimes you really want to stay there.

So, this is where I come through and tell you that you are more than needed. If not by your fellow human being, by the Collectiveness. They have put you on this planet earth to thrive. Get that glimpse of encouragement from the Collectiveness and find what is that you are here for: learning, to **"FEEL GOOD"**. Find your destiny. You are more loved from the invisible that you will ever be loved by the ones that you see around you right now. If you do not know what to do right now, look at the words **"FEEL GOOD"** and start writing things that make you **"FEEL GOOD"**. Gradually you will start to find ways to make you get out of bed in the morning.

If you are in a relationship that doesn't work, find ways to escape. If it is not possible right now, go for walks, little escape weekends. It does work! It will give you strength to do what you believe impossible now.

I believe in you. You have been knitted from greatness. Don't ever forget that.

Lots need to be understood here. So it is your duty to find a teacher. Read books. Ask questions. You deserve better. Believe me.

**A body that is emotionally healthy
does not carry any disease.**

FACTS ABOUT MOTION

Health is like a recipe. When all the ingredients are added, you need to mix the potion... lol.

Some people are looking to get the ultimate program that will make them exercise. But a good walk with the intention of keeping it at the "**FEEL GOOD**" intention is better that any expensive program that you will ever find.

What you need to do when exercising is putting the right intention. Some people exercise to lose weight. Others it's because their doctor told them to do so. But the best exercise that you will ever have is the one that you are doing for the right intent: "**FEELING GOOD**".

If you walk and look at the trees and flowers and occasional critter that comes along, you will benefit your body way much more than going on a one kilometer dash finishing at the end line with being out of breath and all sweaty... lol. Now, don't get me wrong. If you like doing that, go for it. But the one's that I am talking to right now are the one that believe that they need to do exercise because they need to get back into shape, lose weight or have been told by their doctors.

Yes, maybe it is the case but you need to tell yourself that it is to get back to a healthy state of being. Not getting rid of something. You need to find something that you will love doing, not despise. That is the secret of any exercise plan. The intent is the secret.

By moving around, your body fluids will have better facility to expulse toxins. That is the reason of moving around. If you want to run around and you like it and you can, please do. But it is not necessary for the maintenance of your body. We don't need to run away from Dinosaurs any more... lol.

So, after a long day at work, sitting at your desk, go for a nice walk. And remember, don't do it because you have to. Go walk because you want to. Make it fun! Every day, ask yourself: "What new thing am I going to encounter today?"

Also, a body that is well shaken around, will get rid of toxins, and is a healthy body.

Chapter 10

THOU SHALT NOT SPEAK, OR SHOULD I?

When is it time to voice your opinion, or not? We live in a world of make believe, at all time. We need to make believe that what we are doing at work makes a difference. Does it really? We have to follow directives that really if you would look at it, it doesn't even reflect the need of the many, but only the few, and sometime just the one.

We have to drive to jobs that were created mostly for egotistical minds. Interest rates, life insurance, any kind of insurance by the way, expensive cars, expensive anything. If there would be no ego, there would not be a lot of fluff in this world.

Sure there are some commodities. Refrigerators, washers and dryers, a modest car, a modest house. I do not envy others that have more, I'm just saying that there is enough on this planet for everyone. However, it is not well distributed. Everyone on this planet should have a bed to be able to sleep in, food to survive, shelter, and a job to go to, unless you are a mom/dad with kids at home. No one should be paid more than the other since the bread that you buy at the market is the same price for a doctor than the person that is living of the streets. "Life is for living, it isn't a show" like Jim Croce[15] says in a song.

If you do the work for the money, then you are not the doctor that I want working on me. I want a caring person that cares about me. Not a person that works for the pay.

Randy Gage has written a story about the evolution of people kind. (Let's try to stay out of the gender game.) Really enjoyed that story.

It is a story of a shipwreck on an island, somewhat like Gilligan's Island but in a more modern style. People are left to fend for themselves. No shelter, no food. So everyone helps each other building some kind of a hut and create some kind of gadgets to fish and hunt. Every day, everyone have to travel almost a mile to get clean fresh water, until one day, (let's call this guy Goss for the sake of having a name) Goss decides to build, in his spare time, some kind of system with bamboo pipes, that will bring water directly to his hut.

Well then, the fisherperson, the nut gatherer, the hunter and all the other that have started to find ways of making some kind of living, find this invention very good and they suggested to Goss to trade their winnings with him: "I'll give you 2 fishes for a bucket of water", sort of speaking. So everyone that has a trade benefit from each other. This guy is a genius so why not give him things – pay him – to get what he has?

Now, not everyone thinks the same and some do envy

Goss, sitting in the shades all day long, instead of working hard like they are doing. So, they have a meeting and say that everyone should have that commodity at their homes. Goss is willing to build that commodity for them. However, it will cost them. Since Goss is going to have to work all day, building this device and then also maintaining it, he will need to hire people, pay them, and possibly the best way to go about it is to charge everyone some kind of installation fee and then a monthly fee to be able to have that accommodation at their homes.

So, this seems a good plan. Everyone is happy with this and Goss starts the process of building the system to everyone's home. People pay him with all kind of things. He builds a bigger house with all kind of gadgets: a sun roof, a large deck, 3 bedrooms, and a pool in the back (you get the picture?).

But then people start to be envious again about how Goss has more than what they have and they have a meeting again. They say that it is not fair that he gets all the benefits of this deal and they believe that they should have some kind of government that would regulate this system. You know where I am going with this… Because of the envious nature of people, we get ourselves deeper and deeper in debt, to society, and nothing goes anywhere any more.

Any emotion that brings about chaos are to blame here, nothing else. Fear, despair, guilt, jealousy, hatred, revenge, anger, blame, worry, frustration, pessimism and boredom are our enemies.

We need to be content, hopeful, optimistic, believers, happy, passionate, joyful, appreciative, loved and lovable. As a whole, our society doesn't reflect those qualities. So, it is up to each individual to practice and acquire those qualities. And we are not about to get those qualities by reversing them to what was listed before.

The best thing a person can do is to be appreciative for the things that you already have. By envying your neighbour is not the way to go. If you feel that you have been cheated of something, well maybe you were not meant to have it in the first place, or maybe you need to develop skills to get it. There is always choices to make: get the skills to make it or get a better job to buy it. Or, maybe find what should truly be yours. Your lack of something is maybe not what you are looking at right now. Investigate.

I always felt as if there was a lack in my life, as if something was missing, until I learned why we are here. I no more have that feeling. I know that I am part of a whole and if I do not participate in some way to this ratatouille, I will feel that lack again.

So how do you participate? Does it mean that you have to give money? Does it mean that you need to give some time to some kind of organisation? What can you do? As odd as it may seem, living is one of the key element of the participation.

We first need to take care of yourself. Keep us healthy, both physically and mentally, and let's not forget spiritually. To be at par we need to be healthy, wealthy and happy.

Not everyone knows really what those three elements mean. Healthy should be a body that has no parts missing and on no drugs. I fail at that part already. However, I can do the best at what is. Wealthy, for me, means being able to take care of my needs and being able to put some money aside for incidents and vacation time, etc... Modestly at ease is my way of explaining this.

Spiritually means being at last in connection with Source. Knowing that I am never alone, knowing that I am loved. It is an amazing feeling.

My greatest wish is that everyone could feel this way. I didn't say be this way, but feel this way. It doesn't have to be exactly like my world, modest home, etc... Some have mansions and do feel the way I feel. However, we do have some that are considered "up there" that don't really understand the concept I am talking about.

The reason why we have big super markets is because people have stopped fending for themselves. No one has a garden, or a chicken coop, a cow or goats for milk. Many live on land not big enough to have a house and park a car. We stress to work and on our way back home, we buy what is needed for the family. No more big families to take care of the land. Instead of having two parents and many children, we have many parents and few children or equal numbers on both sides.

To give you an example, the granddaughter to my ex-spouse has three sisters and one brother from three different fathers and three different mothers. All conceptions involved drugs, alcohol, or under age pregnancy. This is not judging, these are facts. Catholic religion has been trying to hide these facts for centuries. What is not spoken about, hidden, will continue to happen. If you look in the Bible, these acts were recorded throughout the book. They were spoken about, not hidden. Flesh is a part of us that makes us do things that we either need to ask forgiveness or blame others. It's our choice.

Free will is something that we have to work with. Making a mistake is acceptable and forgivable. Doing the same act over and over again and knowing that it is wrong, and also boasting about it, is not what is going to cure our society. Joking about our wrong doing as been a way that society is accepting as normal. We need to start owning our mistake and accepting consequences.

We have lost the ability to slow down and make the right choice. By right choice I mean whatever will benefit the masses, not only our own egotistical self.

Love is not understood. "We say that we love the baby, but we crucify the man", so well said in on of Jim Croce's songs. If love was not taught to the baby, how can that person show sign of it? So we learn not to tug on Superman's cape, you don't spit into the wind, you don't pull the mask of the old Lone Ranger and you don't mess around with anyone that show any kind of authority.

I wasn't shown any abilities how to defend myself. What I was taught was to turn my tongue seven times in my mouth before answering back to a comment. By that time, the other person was at his or her second or third insult, I only had an answer for the first one. Turn the other cheek was another one that was taught. So, I haven't been able to defend myself and I have always been into situation where people would easily downgrade me in front of others, take advantage of me and then dismissed me like a rag when I was no more needed.

When someone would voice out something inappropriate, my first bodily response was to look mad, but inside I was sad and didn't not know what to answer or say. So, I didn't have friends and I would rather stay alone.

I am not sad being alone. I enjoy my solitude. It is my choice and I like it. Sure sometimes I enjoy the company of people, however I am glad when I am left alone. I don't morn when they are leaving. I don't care about other people's opinion concerning my being. Your opinion of me – or my ways – are of no concern to me.

If you are only around to always telling me my faults, I have no need for you in my life, because I definitively am very well able to downgrade myself since this is what I was taught, at a very young age. My mother was very good at it and I kept her ways a very long time until I understood that it was killing me inside.

I am now able to give myself compliments, I know that I am more than enough, and that I am a very important part of a very big plan. I value myself and others. I have learned how to say no and I also have learn to distance myself from people that are not necessarily needed in my life.

I have finally learned how to love myself. I have also learned to "**FEEL GOOD**" without any help of any one or the possession of something.

I wish this to everyone.

This book, since its creation, has helped me more than once to master the devil. As soon that I feel down, I just grab my book and go through a few pages and I get back to my "**FEEL GOOD**" self. I really hope that it will help you too.

Don't hesitate in filling in the blank pages with "happy thoughts", questions, and anything that might pass through your mind and that you might need some insight.

My publisher asked me a very specific questions which I had to make a decision over. The question was: "Do you believe that you should add some chapters to your book, or should you have a series of book with other pertinent questions?" I chose the latter.

And, I also decided to finish the book with a question, because the book is filled with questions and answers. So, it's kind of going to help you and I to continue this for a while.

So, my question to you is:

"If you would have but one question to ask, what would it be?"

_____

_____

_____

I've got a name - Jim Croce

Like the pine trees lining the winding road
I got a name, I got a name
Like the singing bird and the croaking toad
I got a name, I got a name
And I carry it with me like my daddy did
But I'm living the dream that he kept hid

Moving me down the highway, rolling me down the highway
Moving ahead so life won't pass me by

Like the north wind whistlin' down the sky
I've got a song, I've got a song
Like the whippoorwill and the baby's cry
I've got a song, I've got a song
And I carry it with me and I sing it loud
If it gets me nowhere, I'll go there proud

Moving me down the highway, rolling me down the highway
Moving ahead so life won't pass me by

And I'm gonna go there free

Like the fool I am and I'll always be
I've got a dream, I've got a dream
They can change their minds but they can't change me
I've got a dream, I've got a dream
Oh, I know I could share it if you'd want me to
If you're goin' my way, I'll go with you

Movin' me down the highway, rollin' me down the highway
Movin' ahead so life won't pass me by
Movin' me down the highway, rollin' me down the highway
Movin' ahead so life won't pass me by

IN CONCLUSION, MAYBE THIS BOOK MIGHT BE FOR YOU TOO....

It seems that I needed to add a little something, just as you should put frosting on a cake.

Since December 2017, everything has been spiralling at the speed of light. Source has broken the boundaries of a vicious circle and turned it into a spiralling tornado of possibilities and amazement.

You see, the first three days after I had quit this job at the end of November 2017, I spent them re-reading my journals that I had written for the past ten years and OMG!!! were they all about doom and gloom!!! I saw myself crying until all of a sudden my mind started to say that it was enough! "Enough of the crying, already. You can't continue on this path, it is killing you inside."

This is where I decided to stop writing about martyr and revenge quotes, "bring in the violin and tissue box" stories, and started to write what would be the best things for Carole to do, to get back on track. At that point, I was curing Carole, making Carole a better person. I believe, and it has been told, that it is what you need to do first:

"Take care of yourself first and then go help the world."

Since this project has turned into a manuscript, the only logical thing to do is to give it a logical ending. After re-reading "This book is not for you" many, many times, I have come to the conclusion that it might also be for you too, because it is full of information that can also help you find ways to a better life. Each chapter in itself has a life lesson. Now maybe it is not necessarily exactly what happened to you, however it can be tweaked to your own liking and bring about the adventure that you have been searching for.

It is also showing you how this magnificent body of yours works, and how to take care of it. Some passages might be summarized from other books, but this is what books are supposed to be: summarized in your own understanding so that you can practice the knowledge which you have acquired, and experience it throughout your daily routines and functions. So, like I said all through this book, make it your own. Right notes, underline what made you go AH-HA, and follow those thugs and pulls from Source.

Don't ever stop learning. When you have questions, write them down. You will be amazed in how Source will answer those questions without even any efforts from your part. Slow down. Listen, and wait for the answer. It will come to you, every single time.

Everyone needs to believe that inside us is brewing what needs to be unfolded: a creation, an invention, even a book or two. When it needs to come out, and at the precise moment, it will. You can't rush it! You can't stop it! When it's time it will come to you. And, at that point, it will be but pure amazement.

You are a creation and throughout your stay on this planet earth, you become co-creators. What you need is a glimpse of what you are capable of and to follow that lead.

You are amazing.

You are part of the Divine.

Don't ever let anyone tell you different.

And, keep looking for anything that makes you
"FEEL GOOD".

It is Source's plan for you, always.

ACKNOWLEDGEMENTS

I would like to thank the so many people that have written books, created CD's and DVD's, which has widen my curiosity and has helped me in discovering who Carole really is;

my dad, Edouard Boudreau,

to have encouraged me in reading books

and to never stop dreaming and imagining;

my grandmother, Thérèse Boudreau,

for the love of God

that she has instilled in me;

my grandfather Ernest Boudreau,

to have showed me

what Planet Earth can give us

through gardening and working in the woods.

All three are now walking the realm of invisibility

and are always there to guide me

and find the right way.

I would also like to thank the three Samaritans,

who welcomed me aboard on their trip to the Coffee Shop, in Culver City, USA,

where the seed of publishing this book was planted.

Thanks are also given to so many people who have made this possible.

I will be forever grateful, and will be more alert to the caressing thoughts

planted in my consciousness by Source.

During my never ending journey

through this realm, so misunderstood by so many,

I will do my best to capture and share,

with those interested,

what is offered and revealed to me through my daily meditations.

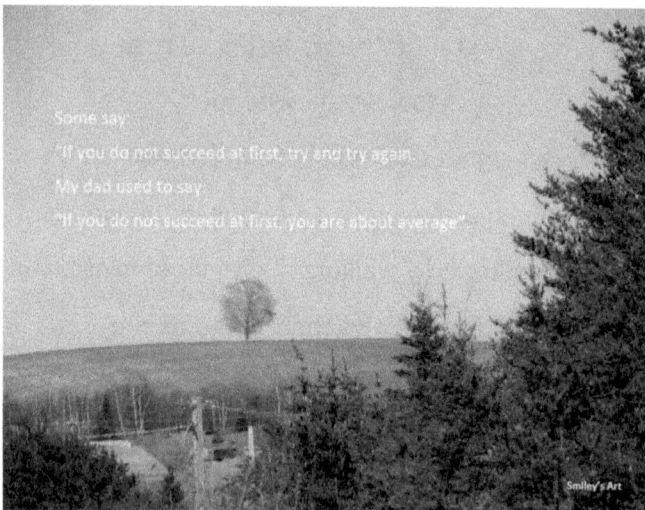

Some say:
"If you do not succeed at first, try and try again."
My dad used to say:
"If you do not succeed at first, you are about average".

Smiley's Art

REFERENCES

1. Michael Bernard Beckwith - https://en.wikipedia.org/wiki/Michael_Beckwith

2. Doctor Joe Dispenza - http://www.drjoedispenza.com

3. Esther Hicks and The Teaching of Abraham - https://en.wikipedia.org/wiki/Esther_Hicks

4. Randy Gage - https://en.wikipedia.org/wiki/Randy_Paul_Gage

5. Why you're dumb, sick and broke - https://www.amazon.com/Youre-Dumb-Broke-Smart-Healthy-ebook/dp/B008L01CVC

6. The secret – you can view this movie on Netflix

7. Rhonda Byrne - https://en.wikipedia.org/wiki/Rhonda_Byrne

8. The matrix - https://en.wikipedia.org/wiki/The_Matrix

9. James Arthur Ray - https://en.wikipedia.org/wiki/James_Arthur_Ray

10. Doctor Joe Vitale - http://www.mrfire.com

11. What the bleep do we know? - https://en.wikipedia.org/wiki/What_the_Bleep_Do_We_Know!%3F

12. Jim Rohn - https://en.wikipedia.org/wiki/Jim_Rohn

13. Doctor Christian Northrup - https://www.drnorthrup.com

14. Edgar Cayce - https://en.wikipedia.org/wiki/Edgar_Cayce

15. Jim Croce - https://en.wikipedia.org/wiki/Jim_Croce

16. Eckhart Tolle - https://en.wikipedia.org/wiki/Eckhart_Tolle

17. The Power of Now - https://en.wikipedia.org/wiki/The_Power_of_Now

www.ingramcontent.com/pod-product-compliance
Lightning Source LLC
La Vergne TN
LVHW051555080426
835510LV00020B/2987